GREAT PLANTS

For GEORGIA GARDENS

# 50

# TREES
# GEORGIA for

# TREES
# GEORGIA
### *for*
#### GREAT PLANTS
#### For GEORGIA GARDENS
#### 50

## *Erica Glasener*
## *Walter Reeves*

**COOL SPRINGS PRESS**

Nashville, Tennessee

A Division of Thomas Nelson, Inc.

www.ThomasNelson.com

Published by Cool Springs Press, a Division of Thomas Nelson, Inc.
P.O. Box 141000, Nashville, Tennessee, 37214.


First printing 2004
Printed in the United States of America
10 9 8 7 6 5 4 3 2 1


Managing Editor: Mary Morgan
Horticulture Editor: Michael Wenzel, Atlanta Botanical Garden
Copyeditor: Michelle Adkerson
Designer: Bill Kersey, Kersey Graphics
Production Artist: S.E. Anderson

On the cover: Franklin Tree, photographed by Jerry Pavia

We gratefully acknowledge the contributions of the following authors who have granted their permission to use selected entries:

American Hornbeam (pg. 14) and Black Gum (pg. 18)—James A. Fizzell; Black Gum (pg. 18)—Ralph Snodsmith; Thornless Honey Locust (pg. 102) and Winter King Hawthorn (pg. 106)—Liz Ball; Chinese Pistachio (pg. 30), Purple Leaf Plum (pg. 80), and Sweet Bay Magnolia (pg. 98)—Dale Groom; Black Gum (pg. 18) and Cornelian Cherry (pg. 32)—Tim Boland, Laura Coit, and Marty Hair; Deodar Cedar (pg. 36)—Toby Bost; Japanese Snowbell (pg. 56), Japanese Stewartia (pg. 58), and Katsura Tree (pg. 62)—Andre Viette and Jacqueline Heriteau; Bald Cypress (pg. 16), Carolina Silverbell (pg. 22), Japanese Zelkova (pg. 60), Ornamental Pear (pg. 72), Serviceberry (pg. 92), Sourwood (pg. 94), Tulip Poplar (pg. 104), and Yellowwood (pg. 108)—Judy Lowe

Visit the Thomas Nelson website at www.ThomasNelson.com

# Table *of* Contents

# How To Use This Book

Each entry in this guide provides you with information about a plant's particular characteristics, habits, and basic requirements for active growth as well as our personal experience and knowledge of the plant. We include the information you need to help you realize each plant's potential. Only when a plant performs at its best can one appreciate it fully. You will find such pertinent information as mature height and spread, bloom period and colors, sun and soil preferences, water requirements, fertilizing needs, pruning and care, and pest information.

## Sun Preferences

Symbols represent the range of sunlight suitable for each plant. Some plants can be grown in more than one range of sun, so you will sometimes see more than one sun symbol.

**Full Sun**

**Part Sun/Shade**

**Full Shade**

## Additional Benefits

Many plants offer benefits that further enhance their appeal. The following symbols indicate some of the more important additional benefits:

 **Attracts Butterflies**

 **Attracts Hummingbirds**

 **Produces Edible Fruit**

 **Has Fragrance**

 **Produces Food for Birds and Wildlife**

 **Drought Resistant**

  **Suitable for Cut Flowers or Arrangements**

 **Long Bloom Period**

 **Native Plant**

 **Supports Bees**

 **Good Fall Color**

**Provides Shelter for Birds**

## Complementary Plants

For many of the entries, we provide landscape design ideas as well as suggestions for companion plants to help you achieve striking and personal gardening results from your garden. This is where we find the most enjoyment from gardening.

## Recommended Selections

This section describes specific cultivars or varieties that are particularly noteworthy. Give them a try.

# 50 Great Trees *for* Georgia

The homes baby boomers bought several years ago have been decorated more than once. Curtains have been hung and rehung. Rooms have been painted and repainted. Furniture has been bought, used, and given to charity. All this may have gone on inside a home while the outside landscape looks the same as it did a decade ago.

Many have realized it's just as creative and enjoyable to decorate outdoors as it is indoors. It's trendy these days to talk about garden *rooms*. Instead of opening the front door and walking onto a one-color, two-dimensional lawn, homeowners have discovered the excitement of walking into an outdoor room with colors and textures that change every day and every season. With good planning, a landscape's yearly change in appearance happens without discarding the old decorations.

Step back from your landscape and think of it as an outdoor room. The trunks of tall trees form the contours of the walls, and their limbs and leaves form a light-filled green ceiling. The smaller, flowering trees supply the paintings that hang on the walls.

A healthy tree enhances your outdoor room, while an unhealthy one degrades it. The following guidelines to growing healthy trees will help you achieve the lovely outdoor room you want.

Ginkgo

## Planting

Over the past twenty years, scientists have done a lot of research on tree planting. Here are three of their conclusions:

1. Adding organic matter to the planting soil for trees makes no difference. In fact, adding amendments may cause the tree roots to remain within the planting hole, where they're vulnerable to drought, rather than extending into the surrounding soil. Roots *will* move

into soil that has lots of oxygen, so the best recommendation is to dig a hole *wide* rather than *deep*, and thoroughly pulverize the soil.

2. The branch tips on small trees produce plant hormones that direct the growth of roots. If you prune a tree to compensate for lost roots, the tree can't tell the roots to begin growing. The best rule is not to prune a tree for a year after planting except to remove damaged limbs or to correct the tree's shape.

3. Roots need lots of calcium and phosphorus to grow well. But spreading lime and fertilizer on top of the soil after a tree is planted is futile—the nutrients dissolve into the root zone too slowly. Add lime and phosphorus to the earth as you shovel it back into the hole, and the roots will be able to use the nutrients immediately.

## *Pruning*

We often hesitate to prune, fearing that such surgery will harm the plant or stunt its growth. While that's an understandable sentiment, it's mistaken. Very rarely does pruning do any permanent damage. Even trees that are pruned at the "wrong" time take little notice of the error.

In general, it's best to remove major limbs from trees anytime from December through February. Light pruning of flowering trees should be done during the first two months after flowering is over. Light pruning of other trees may be done at any time—but never remove more than a quarter of the total foliage.

Unlike animals, plants don't heal, they seal. Once you make a cut, the tree itself internally seals off the damaged area. Don't apply any sealant yourself; let the tree do its work. Tar smeared over a cut eventually dries out and cracks, making a fabulous home for boring insects and diseases. So use your tar to repair the driveway!

Yoshino Cherry

Japanese Zelkova

## Watering

Most of a tree's roots are within 12 inches of the soil's surface. Two weeks of drought and high temperatures in summer will dry the soil and kill small roots. A tree may take years to recover from a prolonged period without water. The best way to ensure the health of your trees is to water them deeply in the summer. Buy a soaker hose and an inexpensive water timer. When daytime temperatures rise above 90 degrees Fahrenheit and no rainfall is expected, water according to these calculations:

| Distance from Trunk to Branch Tips | Gallons of Water per Week |
|:---:|:---:|
| 1 to  5 feet | 8 |
| 5 to 10 feet | 60 |
| 10 to 20 feet | 200 |
| 20 to 35 feet | 750 |
| 35 to 50 feet | 1000 |

In the following pages, we provide the basic information you'll need to select and care for fifty trees that are excellent selections for Georgia. Just keep in mind the eventual mature height and spread of the tree as you decide which ones to buy and where to plant them. Both you and the tree will be happier if it's the right tree in the right place.

# American Holly
## *Ilex opaca*

### *A Splash of Green in the Coldest Weather Plus Bright-Red Berries*

Not all the trees you plant in your yard should be shade trees or flowering trees. Everyone needs at least one evergreen to add a touch of green to the landscape during the dreary months of winter. And what better choice than the native American holly? Just in time for the winter holidays—that season of red and green—it produces bright-crimson berries, providing a naturally decorated tree for your yard.

## Top Reasons to Plant

○ Green in the winter
○ Bright-red berries
○ Good for cutting during winter holidays
○ Effective screen
○ Few bothersome insects or diseases
○ Attractive from indoors in winter

## *Useful Hint*

December is the ideal time to cut holly sprigs and branches to use indoors.

## Bloom Color
White blooms followed by red berries

## Bloom Period
Blooms in spring with berries in fall and winter

## Height/Width
15 to 40 feet x 8 to 30 feet

## Planting Location
- Moist, well-drained, acidic soil
- Full sun or mostly sun

## Planting
- Select a spot that isn't windy.
- For every three to six female hollies, which produce the berries, plant a male that blooms at the same time for pollination—the males and females can be up to 100 feet apart.
- Plant in spring.
- Dig the hole as deep as the rootball and twice as wide.
- Place the tree in the hole and fill in with soil dug from the hole.
- Water well.
- Mulch well.

## Watering
- Water when rainfall is less than an inch weekly.

## Fertilizing
- In early years, fertilize at the end of March or in April using an organic fertilizer such as Holly-tone®.

## Suggestions for Vigorous Growth
- Prune anytime to maintain the pyramidal shape.

# Easy Tip

Place American holly where it can be seen from the street and especially from indoors to view its winter color.

## Pest Control
- Holly leafminers may appear—they leave "trails" in the leaves but generally aren't harmful.
- Scale is sometimes a problem—it looks like tiny brown bumps on the stems and undersides of leaves.
- Adult spittlebugs, black insects with two red stripes, may damage leaves.
- If any of these are serious infestations, consult the Extension Service about controls.

## Complementary Plants
- Use several American hollies together for screening or a windbreak.

## Recommended Selections
- 'Jersey Princess' has lustrous dark-green leaves ('Jersey Knight' is the male pollinator).
- Hybrid hollies such as 'Fosteri', 'Nellie R. Stevens', 'Emily Bruner', and 'James Swan' are proven performers.

# American Hornbeam

*Carpinus caroliniana*

### A Tough Native Tree That Tolerates a Variety of Conditions

American hornbeam is a tough native of the bottomlands. It tolerates wet or dry, acidic or alkaline soils, and sunny or shaded situations. Hornbeam is attractive year-round. The catkins are light-green as leaves begin to open. The leaves are small enough to allow the interesting structure of the tree to show through. Fall color is yellow to orange. And in winter, the beautiful smooth, gray bark on multiple, muscular trunks is quite handsome.

## Top Reasons to Plant

○ Four seasons of interest
○ Grows well under the shade of larger trees
○ Good fall color
○ Muscular structure
○ Smooth, gray bark attractive in winter
○ Relatively small
○ Few bothersome insects and diseases
○ Good shelter for birds

## Useful Hint

Put American hornbeam where you can appreciate its interesting four-season character.

14

## Bloom Color
Light-green

## Bloom Period
Spring

## Height/Width
20 feet x 20 feet

## Planting Location
- Prefers moist, well-drained soil, but tolerates alkalinity and other difficult situations
- Sun to partial shade

## Planting
- Transplant balled-and-burlapped trees when they are small.
- Plant in spring.
- Site no closer than 10 feet to a structure.
- Dig the hole a little shallower than the rootball and twice as wide.
- Set the tree in the hole, and remove the burlap.
- Fill the hole with original soil.
- Water well.
- Use any remaining soil to make a saucer around the tree.

## Watering
- Water during extended dry periods.

## Easy Tip

American hornbeam is especially useful on a site where larger, overhanging trees cast shade and keep the soil moist.

## Fertilizing
- No fertilizer is needed.

## Suggestions for Vigorous Growth
- Prune if you prefer, but American hornbeam seldom needs it.

## Pest Control
- No serious pests or diseases trouble this tree.

## Complementary Plants
- American hornbeam works best as a specimen shade tree.

## Recommended Selections
- Plant the native species rather than a cultivar.

# Bald Cypress
*Taxodium distichum*

## A Native with Needles That Change Color in Autumn

Most of us think of trees that have needles as evergreen and of trees that have leaves as deciduous (losing their foliage in fall). Bald cypress completely upsets those beliefs—it's a tree with needles, but they become a wonderful cinnamon color in autumn and then fall off. Trees like this are called deciduous conifers—they bear cones, like evergreens, but the needles fall in winter, like most trees with leaves.

## Top Reasons to Plant

- Beautiful shedding bark
- Tolerates most soils
- Good cover for birds
- Pleasant fragrance
- Few bothersome insects and diseases
- Lovely fall color

## Useful Hint

Place this tree where its shedding bark can be admired.

## Bloom Color
Purplish drooping clusters

## Bloom Period
Early spring

## Height/Width
50 to 85 feet x 18 to 65 feet

## Planting Location
- Ideal for boggy, acidic soil but tolerates almost any type of soil that isn't alkaline
- Sun

## Planting
- Plant in early fall or in spring.
- Allow plenty of space—this tree grows very large.
- Dig the hole the same depth as the rootball and twice as wide.
- Place the tree in the hole and fill in with soil dug from the hole.
- Mulch well, keeping mulch 2 inches away from trunk.

## Watering
- Water weekly for the first two years.
- After two years, no additional watering is needed.

## Fertilizing
- During the first few years, fertilize each fall after the needles have fallen; use a high-nitrogen fertilizer according to package directions.

## Easy Tip

Bald cypress thrives in a permanently wet spot in the yard, but it also does well with average moisture.

## Suggestions for Vigorous Growth
- Yellowing needles probably indicate soil that's not acidic enough—spray with chelated iron and use fertilizer for acid-loving plants.
- Don't worry about knobby growths at the base; these "knees" are normal in wet sites.
- Prune dead branches anytime.

## Pest Control
- If bagworms appear, pick them off by hand.
- Spray the tree with water if spider mites cause the needles to turn brown anytime except fall.

## Complementary Plants
- This large tree works best as a specimen with plenty of space.

## Recommended Selections
- 'Apache Chief' is a handsome, wide-spreading tree.

# Black Gum
*Nyssa sylvatica*

## A Beautiful Native with Fine Fall Foliage

One of our finest native trees, black gum has a distinctive pyramidal form, good branching, and excellent fall color. It consistently provides a fall display of brilliant scarlet, yellow, orange, and purple leaves. In summer, it has lustrous, shiny green foliage. While it prefers swampy places, black gum is found growing in upland sites, woodlots, and abandoned farmlands. Its dark-blue fruits, about ¹/₄ inch in diameter, attract birds.

## Top Reasons to Plant

○ Outstanding fall color
○ Excellent summer foliage
○ Provides food and shelter for birds
○ Few bothersome pests and diseases
○ Loves wet, swampy sites
○ Grass can grow beneath the limbs

## Useful Hint

While the flowers are barely noticeable to humans, bees adore them, and Tupelo honey (black gum is also known as black tupelo) is a popular southern favorite.

## Bloom Color
White flowers but not showy

## Bloom Period
Spring

## Height/Width
50 feet x 30 feet

## Planting Location
- Deep, well-drained acidic soil
- Full sun or a little shade

## Planting
- Plant only in spring before new growth starts; black gum can be difficult to transplant.
- Dig the hole no deeper than the rootball and twice as wide.
- Place the tree in the hole and fill in with soil dug from the hole.
- If tree is balled and burlapped, remove the burlap and place the tree in the hole.
- Water well.
- Form a saucer around the plant with any remaining soil.

## Watering
- During the first year, water regularly, keeping the roots moist.
- When the tree is established, water thoroughly at least once a month during periods of drought.

*Easy Tip*

Choose plants in containers or smaller trees; black gum can be tricky to transplant due to its long tap-root.

## Fertilizing
- Each year, top-dress using an acid-based mulch, or in spring, apply fertilizer formulated for acid-loving trees.

## Suggestions for Vigorous Growth
- Do not prune or otherwise disrupt the main trunk or stem; this damages the tree's natural form.

## Pest Control
- Few pests or diseases bother this tree.
- Yellowing leaves may be due to the soil not being acidic enough—feed with acidic fertilizer.

## Complementary Plants
- Black gum makes an excellent specimen tree for lawns.

## Recommended Selections
- 'Jermyn's Flame' has larger leaves than the species.

# Canadian Hemlock

*Tsuga canadensis*

*A Graceful, Stately Evergreen for the Northern Third of the State*

In Georgia, we have only a narrow range of needled trees to provide contrast in form and color to our many broadleafed trees. We do find Canadian hemlock, though, in the northern third of the state. This excellent evergreen is exceptionally graceful and has several uses in the landscape. It may be pruned as a hedge or allowed to grow into a tall, stately pyramid to screen the disarray in your neighbor's backyard.

## Top Reasons to Plant

- Tolerates heat and humidity
- Thrives in shade or filtered shade
- Graceful form
- Green all year
- Grows quickly
- Good hedge or screen

## Useful Hint

Both excellent drainage and regular watering during the summer are essential for Canadian hemlock.

## Bloom Color
Prized for its deep-green, soft-textured foliage

## Bloom Period
Foliage effective year-round

## Height/Width
40 to 70 feet x 25 to 40 feet

## Planting Location
- Moist but well-drained soil preferably containing lots of organic matter
- Tolerates sun with frequent watering; partial shade is ideal, but full shade is okay

## Planting
- Plant in midautumn or early spring.
- Dig the hole as deep as the rootball and twice as wide.
- In clay soil where drainage is a problem, dig the hole five times as wide as the rootball, adding to the soil 10 pounds of pea gravel and 1 cubic foot of soil conditioner for every foot of hole diameter.
- Add 1 cup of lime and 1 tablespoon of 0-46-0 fertilizer per foot of hole diameter.
- Place the tree in the hole and cut away all visible burlap, twine, or wire.
- Fill the hole with soil dug from the hole or use improved soil in areas with clay.
- Water well.
- Mulch with 2 inches of pine straw or wood chips.

## Watering
- Water regularly to keep the soil moist, especially when the tree is getting established and during hot spells.

*Easy Tip*

If you're planting a hemlock in dense shade, purchase the largest tree you can afford—growth is slower in very shady locations.

## Fertilizing
- In March, May, and September, feed young trees 1 cup of 10-10-10 fertilizer for every inch of thickness of the trunk 4 feet above the ground.
- Mature trees rarely need fertilizer.

## Suggestions for Vigorous Growth
- If using the tree as a hedge or screen, shear it in spring or summer for a formal look or thin the branches for a more informal appearance.

## Pest Control
- Few hemlock pests have reached Georgia—its worst enemy here is the environment.

## Complementary Plants
- Plant with shade-loving shrubs, such as evergreen azalea, rhododendron, mountain laurel, and oakleaf hydrangea.

## Recommended Selections
- 'Sargentii' is a beautiful weeping form that grows about 10 feet high and 15 feet wide.
- Carolina hemlock (*Tsuga caroliniana*) may be hardier in Georgia landscapes.

21

# Carolina Silverbell

*Halesia tetraptera*

## A Charming Native with Graceful Clusters of Spring Blooms

Most southerners have a special fondness for spring-flowering trees, as witnessed by practically every neighborhood's being filled with dogwoods and redbuds. Carolina silverbell fits right into this trend. It's a charming native tree with graceful white or pink bell-shaped blooms hanging in delicate clusters along the branches in mid- to late spring before the leaves appear, and fruits that last into winter.

## Top Reasons to Plant

- Beautiful spring flowers
- Fruits that last into winter
- Insect and disease resistant
- Requires little care
- Good alternative to flowering dogwood

## Useful Hint

Try to situate Carolina silverbell on a hill or slope so the flowers can be viewed from below.

## Bloom Color
White or pink

## Bloom Period
Spring

## Height/Width
30 to 50 feet x 20 to 35 feet

## Planting Location
- Moist, acidic soil that drains well and contains lots of organic matter
- Partial shade for best results, but will tolerate more sun

## Planting
- Choose container-grown plants rather than balled-and-burlapped ones.
- Plant in early fall or in spring.
- Dig the hole as deep as the rootball and twice as wide.
- Place the tree in the hole and fill in with soil dug from the hole.
- Water well.
- Mulch well.

## Watering
- Water often enough to keep the soil moist—do not let it dry out.

## Fertilizing
- Fertilizer is not needed except when the tree is young.
- If the tree is not growing well, spread a high-nitrogen fertilizer for trees in a wide circle around the trunk after the leaves fall in autumn.

*Easy Tip*

Experts recommend planting Carolina silverbell where dogwoods can't grow because of leaf disease.

## Suggestions for Vigorous Growth
- Renew mulch as needed.
- Begin training the tree to a single trunk when it's young—otherwise, it becomes a large shrub, which isn't as attractive.
- Prune—never removing more than one-fourth of the growth in one year—in spring, after flowering.

## Pest Control
- This tree resists insects and diseases well.

## Complementary Plants
- Use as a nice understory tree with pines.
- For an attractive display, combine with lily-of-the-valley, evergreen azalea, rhododendron, and with other spring-flowering trees.

## Recommended Selections
- 'Rosea' has pink flowers.
- 'Arnold Pink' has larger flowers than those on the species.

# Chaste Tree

*Vitex agnus-castus*

## A Showy Small Tree with Spectacular Blue Blossoms

During the Summer Olympics, visitors to the Georgia Agricultural Pavilion at Centennial Olympic Park always stopped in surprise before the chaste tree on display— it looked so much like a butterfly bush, but it obviously wasn't. Georgia gardeners are rapidly discovering this small tree or large shrub, with its light-green leaves topped in midsummer by 6-inch, light-blue flower spikes. It's an excellent centerpiece in the landscape.

### Top Reasons to Plant

○ Beautiful blue blossoms in summer
○ Fragrant flowers
○ Airy form
○ Can be trained as shrub or small tree
○ Compact size
○ Tolerates heat and humidity
○ Insect and disease resistant

## Useful Hint

With the lower limbs trimmed off, chaste tree turns from a large shrub into an airy shade tree.

## Bloom Color
Blue, lavender, white, or pink

## Bloom Period
Summer

## Height/Width
8 to 25 feet x 15 to 20 feet

## Planting Location
- Prefers well-drained soil
- Full sun

## Planting
- If you're not planning to prune it into a tree shape, place 20 feet from other plants.
- Plant in spring in north Georgia and fall in south Georgia.
- Dig the hole as deep as the rootball and twice as wide.
- Place the plant in the hole and water with transplanting solution to stimulate root growth.
- Fill in around roots with soil from the hole.
- Water well.
- Mulch well.

## Watering
- During the first two years, water deeply whenever rainfall is less than an inch each week.
- When established, this plant can tolerate dry conditions, but it grows best with regular water.

## Fertilizing
- For the first two years after planting, feed the tree in March, May, and July with 1 tablespoon of 10-10-10 fertilizer per foot of plant height.

## *Easy Tip*

Chaste tree's small size, interesting foliage, and late-season bloom make it an excellent patio tree as long as you don't mind the bees that love it.

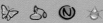

- Once the tree is established, feed with 1 tablespoon of 10-10-10 per foot of plant height in April and June.

## Suggestions for Vigorous Growth
- Remove lower limbs in very early spring to train to a tree shape.
- Prune to remove winter damage at the same time.
- In north Georgia, winter cold may freeze most of the limbs—if it does, cut the plant back to 12 inches tall.

## Pest Control
- In very rainy weather, leaf spots may appear but they usually aren't serious.
- Few other insect or disease problems bother this tree.

## Complementary Plants
- At the Georgia Agricultural Pavilion, chaste tree was planted with 'Zuni' crapemyrtles on each side and 'New Gold' lantana covering the ground in front.

## Recommended Selections
- *Vitex agnus-castus* 'Latifolia' has larger leaves and flowers longer.
- 'Alba' has white flowers.

# Cherry Laurel
*Prunus caroliniana*

## A Shade Lover with Deep-Green Foliage Needing Little Care

Occasionally, a cherry laurel offers the only solution to a difficult landscape situation. It tolerates more shade than any other broadleafed tree and grows relatively fast even in shade. Some object to cherry laurel's small purple berries that appear in copious quantities in October, much to the delight of native birds. They can't digest the hard seeds inside the fruit, and cherry laurel seedlings spring up wherever birds alight. But unlike oak seedlings, they're a snap to pull up and remove in spring.

## Top Reasons to Plant

- Thrives in shade
- Evergreen in most parts of the state
- Requires little care
- Makes excellent thick screen, hedge, or windbreak
- Few pests or diseases
- Attracts birds

## Useful Hint

In the coldest parts of Georgia, cherry laurel may lose its leaves in winter or may even be frozen to the ground.

## Bloom Color
White flowers, followed by black berries

## Bloom Period
Early spring

## Height/Width
20 to 30 feet x 15 to 20 feet

## Planting Location
- Prefers moist, well-drained soils but tolerates a variety of conditions
- Sun or shade

## Planting
- Plant in midautumn or early spring.
- Dig the planting hole three to five times as wide and the same depth as the rootball.
- Add 1 cup of lime and 1 tablespoon of 0-46-0 fertilizer per foot of hole diameter.
- Place the plant in the hole and remove any burlap, twine, or wire.
- Fill the hole with soil dug from the hole.
- Water thoroughly.
- Mulch with 2 inches of pine straw or wood chips.

## Watering
- Water heavily every week if temperatures rise above 95 degrees Fahrenheit.

## Fertilizing
- While the tree is young, feed it in March, May, and September with 1 cup of 10-10-10 fertilizer for each inch of trunk thickness measured 4 feet above the ground.
- Once the tree matures, little fertilizer is needed.

## *Easy Tip*
Be sure to leave enough room to maneuver underneath the trees so you can pull up the seedlings each year.

## Suggestions for Vigorous Growth
- Prune to a tree shape or a thick rounded hedge.
- To keep foliage growing densely in shade, prune off branch tips every March.

## Pest Control
- Few insect or disease problems trouble this tree.
- If hundreds of tiny holes appear in the leaves, the plant probably has the bacterial disease called "shothole," which is best prevented by keeping the foliage dry.

## Complementary Plants
- Cherry laurel is typically used as a hedge, screen, or windbreak—plant trees 6 to 10 feet apart for that purpose.

## Recommended Selections
- 'Bright 'N Tight'™ has leaves smaller than those of the species, and the foliage is dense.
- 'Cherry Ruffles' grows to 15 feet and has deep-green, ruffled leaves.

# Chinese Elm
*Ulmus parvifolia*

## A Disease-Resistant Elm with Fabulous Bark

Elms were once the predominant street tree in cities through the Northeast and Midwest. When the European bark beetle arrived on this continent and began spreading Dutch elm disease, millions of elms began to die. One of the best substitutes is the Chinese elm. Though smaller than the American elm, it has similar ascending branches and resists pests. Its bark is striking—small patches drop off to form a beautiful, mottled combination of gray, green, and brown.

## Top Reasons to Plant

- Beautiful showy bark in winter
- Disease and insect resistant
- Good fall color
- Adaptable to varying soils
- Tough and durable
- Excellent shade tree

## *Useful Hint*

Don't confuse this tree with Siberian elm (*Ulmus pumila*), a fast-growing tree that is *not* recommended.

## Bloom Color
Inconsequential

## Bloom Period
Late summer

## Height/Width
40 to 50 feet x 40 to 50 feet

## Planting Location
- Well-drained soil, either acidic or alkaline, but best results are in moist soil with organic matter
- Full sun

## Planting
- Plant in midautumn or early spring.
- Dig the hole as deep as the rootball and three to five times as wide.
- Add 1 cup of lime and 1 tablespoon of 0-46-0 fertilizer per foot of hole diameter.
- Place the tree in the hole and remove any twine, wire, or burlap.
- Fill with dirt dug from the hole.
- Mulch with 2 inches of pine straw or wood chips.

## Watering
- When the tree is young, water regularly when rainfall doesn't amount to an inch per week.
- If summer temperatures rise above 95 degrees Fahrenheit, water heavily each week.

## Fertilizing
- While the tree is young, feed it in March, May, and September with 1 cup of 10-10-10 fertilizer for each inch of trunk thickness measured 4 feet above the ground.
- Once the tree matures, fertilizer is usually not needed.

## Easy Tip

Chinese elm grows rapidly, so place it an appropriate distance away from structures or other plants.

## Suggestions for Vigorous Growth
- After the tree reaches moderate size, remove one or two of the lowest limbs each winter until the lowest limbs are at least 8 feet off the ground.
- If the tree needs support, place a stake 18 inches away from both sides of the trunk and attach the stakes in a way that allows the tree to sway slightly.

## Pest Control
- This tree resists diseases and pests.

## Complementary Plants
- Chinese elm makes an excellent specimen tree where its bark can be seen and appreciated; its deep-green leaves make a nice contrast in front of a large, red brick home.

## Recommended Selections
- 'Athena' was selected by the Georgia Gold Medal Plant Committee as a superior tree that deserves to be used more often.
- 'Alee'® has an upright, arching crown similar to that of the American elm.
- 'Burgundy' has good purple fall foliage.

29

# Chinese Pistachio

*Pistacia chinensis*

## A Versatile Small Tree with Outstanding Fall Color

An excellent small- to medium-sized tree, Chinese pistachio tolerates a wide range of locations and soil conditions. Once established, it is deep rooted and drought tolerant. It also offers reliable fall color even in the mildest areas of the state, with beautiful yellow, red-orange, and red leaves. Its wood is very strong, so wind and ice do little damage.

## Top Reasons to Plant

- ○ Adapts to a wide range of soils
- ○ Beautiful fall foliage
- ○ Drought tolerant when established
- ○ Turf can grow beneath it
- ○ Pest and disease resistant
- ○ Grows quickly

## Useful Hint

Chinese pistachio tolerates hot, confined areas.

## Bloom Color
Non-showy spring bloom

## Bloom Period
Fall foliage in yellow, red-orange, and red; thick heads of small, reddish brown fruit or seeds in fall

## Height/Width
20 to 40 feet x 20 to 30 feet

## Planting Location
- Prefers moist, well-drained soil but tolerates a wide range of conditions
- Sun

## Planting
- Plant container-grown stock in fall or early spring.
- Dig the hole as deep as the rootball and twice as wide.
- Place the tree in the hole and water with a transplant solution.
- Fill with soil dug from the hole.
- Mulch well.

## Watering
- Water regularly until established.
- This tree tolerates drought once established but grows faster with regular watering.

## Fertilizing
- No fertilizer is required, but the tree grows more quickly with regular fertilizer.

## *Easy Tip*
Chinese pistachio grows quickly when fertilized and watered regularly.

- For fastest growth, feed three to four times a year—early spring, eight weeks later, eight weeks after that, and once in fall—with a balanced, slow-release fertilizer.

## Suggestions for Vigorous Growth
- Prune as needed when the tree is young to train growth.

## Pest Control
- No serious pests or diseases trouble this tree.

## Complementary Plants
- Use in an informal naturalized grouping or as a specimen tree.

## Recommended Selections
- There are no known cultivars, so plant the species.

# Cornelian Cherry

*Cornus mas*

## An Excellent Small Tree Blooming in Very Early Spring

Every spring as we wait for the first flowers and other signs winter is ending, this surprisingly early-blooming dogwood bursts into flower on leafless branches. Its bright-yellow flowers cover the tree *en masse*, making it noticeable even from a distance. Summer months bring lustrous green foliage, and by August, red cherrylike fruits appear. In full sun, the fall color is reddish purple, and in winter, the flaky bark is interesting.

## Top Reasons to Plant

- Offers interest in four seasons
- Beautiful yellow blooms in very early spring
- Bright-red fruits and purple leaves in fall
- Flaking bark in winter
- Attracts birds

## Useful Hint

Cornelian cherry isn't recommended for coastal gardens in Georgia—it needs cooler weather in both winter and summer.

## Bloom Color
Yellow

## Bloom Period
Early spring

## Height/Width
20 to 25 feet x 15 to 20 feet

## Planting Location
- Adapts to most soil types except very wet or very dry
- Prefers sun for best growth and flowers, but tolerates light shade

## Planting
- Plant in spring—fall planting is less successful.
- Dig the hole as deep as the rootball and twice as wide.
- Place the plant in the hole and fill in with soil dug from the hole.
- Water well.
- Mulch well.

## Watering
- Keep roots moist until established.

## Fertilizing
- No fertilizer is required.

## *Easy Tip*
Cut branches of cornelian cherry in winter, put them in a vase on a warm windowsill, and you'll have fresh blooms for the house.

## Suggestions for Vigorous Growth
- Nursery plants are available as single-stem trees or multistem shrubs.
- Prune only to remove dead, diseased, or dying branches.
- On older specimens, prune to remove crowded growth.
- Bloom is showiest and growth most vigorous in colder parts of the state.

## Pest Control
- No serious insects or diseases bother this plant.

## Complementary Plants
- Cornelian cherry is stunning massed against a backdrop of dark-needled evergreens.

## Recommended Selections
- 'Golden Glory' features an upright form with heavy flowering.
- 'Variegata' has leaves mottled with creamy-white markings.

# Dawn Redwood
## *Metasequoia glyptostroboides*

## An Ancient Fast-Growing Conifer for a Larger Landscape

Dawn redwood was found growing wild in China in 1941, but the fossil record shows this tree is millions of years old. When you look at a dawn redwood, imagine pterodactyls flying above and a brontosaurus munching on nearby giant ferns. That was dawn redwood's era. Today, it makes an excellent fast-growing shade tree for a larger landscape. Its leaves are soft needles 1/2-inch long, and they fall from the tree each autumn after turning russet.

## Top Reasons to Plant

- Fast-growing
- Symmetrical cone shape without pruning
- Good shade tree
- Loses needles in winter, allowing sun through
- No serious pests or diseases
- Interesting history—dates back to the dinosaurs

## Bloom Color
Prized for its soft green needles in summer, turning orange-brown in fall

## Bloom Period
Foliage effective spring through fall

## Height/Width
70 to 100 feet x 15 to 25 feet

## Planting Location
• Slightly acidic, well-drained soil that holds moisture
• Sun

## Planting
• Plant a balled-and-burlapped tree in midautumn or early spring.
• Dig the hole as deep as the rootball and three to five times as wide.
• Add 1 cup lime and 1 tablespoon of 0-46-0 fertilizer per foot of hole diameter.
• Place the tree in the hole and cut away all burlap, twine, or wire.
• Fill in with soil dug from the hole.
• Water well.
• Mulch with 2 inches of pine straw or wood chips.

## Watering
• Water regularly until established.
• If summer temperatures rise above 95 degrees Fahrenheit, water heavily each week.

*Easy Tip*

Dawn redwood can grow 4 feet per year under good conditions.

## Fertilizing
• Apply small amounts of fertilizer regularly to help a young tree grow throughout summer.
• Measure the thickness of the trunk 4 feet from the ground, and in March, May, and September, apply 1 cup of 10-10-10 fertilizer for each inch of trunk thickness.
• Once the tree matures, little fertilizer is needed.

## Suggestions for Vigorous Growth
• Light pruning can be done anytime.
• If the young tree needs support, a stake placed 18 inches away from both sides of the trunk will keep it upright, but stake the tree so it can sway slightly.

## Pest Control
• No serious pests or diseases bother this tree.

## Complementary Plants
• Use as a specimen tree in a very large open area.

## Recommended Selections
• There are no cultivars, so plant the species.

*Useful Hint*

Dawn redwood commands a lot of space, so don't plant it unless you can give it the room it needs.

# Deodar Cedar
*Cedrus deodara*

## A Graceful Evergreen That Makes a Strong Statement

Deodar cedar is a marvelous tree for the landscape on larger properties where evergreens are not cramped for space. Mature specimens look like distant mountains on the horizon. These trees mature at 70 feet, and their wide-spreading pyramidal form makes a statement wherever you plant them. But don't crowd them into small yards—neither they nor you will be happy with the results.

## Top Reasons to Plant

○ Beautiful, graceful evergreen
○ Wide-spreading, pyramidal form
○ Excellent for large, open areas
○ Fine texture and soft look
○ Drought tolerant when established
○ Tolerates heat and humidity
○ Grows relatively quickly

## Useful Hint

Deodar cedar is an excellent choice for hot, humid areas.

## Bloom Color
Prized for its dark-green, evergreen foliage

## Bloom Period
Foliage effective year-round

## Height/Width
70 feet x 40 feet

## Planting Location
- Well-drained, somewhat dry soil
- Sun or half shade

## Planting
- Plant container-grown trees from spring through early fall.
- Dig the hole as deep as the rootball and twice as wide.
- Add a fertilizer planting tablet to the hole or add $1/4$ cup superphosphate.
- Place the tree in the hole and fill with soil dug from the hole.
- Water thoroughly.
- Mulch well.

## Watering
- Water three times the first week, twice the second week, then once every seven to ten days until strong new growth begins.
- Once established, this tree tolerates dry soils.

## Fertilizing
- In spring of the second growing season, apply a general garden fertilizer.
- Every two or three years thereafter, fertilize in spring.

## Easy Tip
Deodar cedar's fine texture and needlelike leaves make a pleasing backdrop for broadleaf shrub borders.

## Suggestions for Vigorous Growth
- Do not prune or stake unless there's good reason to do so.
- As the tree matures, some lower limbs die, which is natural.
- Do not try to grow grass inside the drip line of the tree—leave it mulched.

## Pest Control
- No serious insects or diseases bother this tree.

## Complementary Plants
- Due to its stature, use deodar cedar as a specimen tree.

## Recommended Selections
- 'Shalimar' is the most cold hardy.
- 'Aurea' has new foliage that's yellow in spring and turns golden-green as it matures.
- 'Compacta', a slow-growing cultivar, reaches about 15 feet tall in twenty years.
- 'Pendula', a weeping form, grows very low to the ground.

# Florida Maple

*Acer barbatum*

## A Georgia Alternative to the Brilliant Sugar Maple

The Florida maple is similar to the sugar maple, but it's smaller and grows much better in our sweltering heat. While sugar maples grown south of Macon down to the Florida line will suffer during summer, the Florida maple thrives all the way to north Florida. Its fall color is a bright-yellow most people find pleasing. When grown in the open, the Florida maple's trunk is short, and its limbs naturally form a graceful oval.

## Top Reasons to Plant

- Beautiful fall color
- Thrives in heat and humidity
- Excellent shade tree
- Smaller than sugar maple
- Few pests and diseases

## *Useful Hint*

Florida maple is sometimes affected by air pollution, so don't plant it near a busy street.

## Bloom Color
Grown for its foliage

## Bloom Period
Foliage is effective summer through fall

## Height/Width
20 to 25 feet x 20 to 25 feet

## Planting Location
- Prefers moist, well-drained soils but will tolerate drier situations
- Sun or light shade

## Planting
- Plant balled-and-burlapped trees or container-grown trees in midautumn or early spring.
- Dig the hole three to five times the width of and the same depth as the rootball.
- Add 1 cup of lime and 1 tablespoon of 0-46-0 fertilizer per foot of hole diameter.
- Set the tree in the hole and cut away all burlap, twine, or wire.
- Fill with soil dug from the hole.
- Water well.
- Mulch with 2 inches of pine straw or wood chips.

## Watering
- Water regularly while the tree is young.
- Once the tree is established, water heavily each week if summer temperatures rise above 95 degrees Fahrenheit.

## Fertilizing
- While the tree is young, feed it in March, May, and September with 1 cup of 10-10-10 fertilizer for each inch of

## Easy Tip
Some scientists believe the Florida maple is just a smaller variety of sugar maple—whether that's true or not, it's a fine tree for most parts of Georgia.

trunk thickness measured 4 feet above the ground.
- Once the tree matures, little fertilizer is needed.

## Suggestions for Vigorous Growth
- Prune lightly at any time.
- If the young tree needs support, a stake placed 18 inches away from both sides of the trunk will keep it upright, but stake the tree so it can sway slightly.

## Pest Control
- Japanese beetles sometimes chew on Florida maple leaves—ask your Extension Agent about appropriate controls.
- Leaf scorch or sun scald may affect young trees if they aren't watered regularly for the first year.

## Complementary Plants
- This tree is best used as a specimen shade tree in the lawn.

## Recommended Selections
- There are no known cultivars, so plant the species.

# Flowering Crabapple

*Malus* species and cultivars

## A Very Showy Spring Bloomer— but Handle with Care

Flowering crabapples are seductive trees, with showy spring blossoms followed by small red, orange, or yellow fruits beloved by birds and which sometimes hang onto the tree until after the leaves drop. But be warned—crabapples are very disease prone, so purchase only named cultivars that are known to do well in your area. Otherwise, you'll spend lots of time spraying or being unhappy with your sickly tree—or both. But the right crabapple will create a beautiful focal point in your yard.

## Top Reasons to Plant

- Beautiful spring flowers
- Handsome fruit
- Nice winter silhouette
- Compact scale good for small areas and one-story houses
- The right cultivar requires little care

## Useful Hint

If you have an outside eating area and enjoy birds, plant a flowering crabapple where you can see it from the window; you'll enjoy the blooms, fruits, and foliage—as well as the visiting birds.

40

## Bloom Color
White, pink, red, or blends

## Bloom Period
Spring

## Height/Width
10 to 20 feet x 15 to 25 feet

## Planting Location
- Prefers deep, fertile, moist soils but tolerates most soil types
- Sun

## Planting
- Plant in midautumn or early spring.
- Dig the hole three times as wide as and the same depth as the rootball.
- Using a spade, pulverize the clods of earth in the hole.
- Place the tree in the hole and remove any burlap, twine, or wire.
- Fill the hole with soil dug from the hole.
- Water well.
- Mulch with 2 inches of shredded bark, fine bark, or pine straw.

## Watering
- Water regularly until the tree is established.
- Water deeply during drought periods.

## Fertilizing
- For the first few years, fertilize in April and late June using $1/8$ cup of 10-10-10 fertilizer for each foot of tree height.

## Suggestions for Vigorous Growth
- One month after planting, inspect the tree to see whether the soil has settled and exposed the top surface of the rootball—if so, add more soil.

*Easy Tip*

Plant only named cultivars of crabapples that have proven disease-resistant in your part of the state.

- Prune in spring to maintain a rounded form and to remove pencil-sized "water sprouts."
- Do not prune heavily after early June, or you'll remove next year's flowers.

## Pest Control
- Few insect problems trouble this tree.
- Disease problems—unless you have a disease-resistant cultivar—include fireblight, powdery mildew, apple scab, and cedar-apple rust. Always plant disease-resistant cultivars.

## Complementary Plants
- Group three flowering crabapples in a triangular pattern in a sunny corner of the yard.
- Plant in beds with annuals or perennials.

## Recommended Selections
- 'Callaway' was selected as a markedly superior tree at Callaway Gardens.
- 'Donald Wyman' and 'Dolgo' are almost as disease resistant as 'Callaway'.

# Flowering Dogwood

*Cornus florida*

### The Ultimate Spring-Flowering Tree for Georgia

Is there any tree more strongly associated with spring in Georgia than the flowering dogwood? In mid-April when azaleas and dogwoods are at their peak, Georgia enchants out-of-state visitors. The white flower bracts glow in spring, and the bright-red berries that follow are attractive in September while the leaves are still on the tree. Seeds that survive the squirrels are spread by birds and will grow wherever conditions are favorable.

## Top Reasons to Plant

○ Beautiful clouds of spring flowers
○ Bright-red fall color
○ Late-summer red berries that attract birds
○ Interesting bark
○ Attractive layered habit
○ Says "spring" like no other tree

## Useful Hint

Underplant your dogwood with low-growing spring-flowering shrubs—they not only look pretty, but discourage damage to the dogwood from mowers and string trimmers.

## Bloom Color
White, pink, or red

## Bloom Period
Spring

## Height/Width
10 to 20 feet x 10 to 25 feet

## Planting Location
- Moist, acidic, well-drained soil with lots of organic matter—avoid poorly drained soil
- Prefers partial shade; the best site is on the eastern or northern side of larger trees or a house to provide shelter from the hot sun

## Planting
- Plant in midautumn or early spring.
- Dig the hole three to five times as wide as and the same depth as the rootball.
- Add 1 cup of lime and 1 tablespoon of 0-46-0 fertilizer per foot of hole diameter.
- Place the tree in the hole and cut away all visible burlap, twine, or wire.
- Fill with soil from the hole.
- Water thoroughly.
- Mulch with 2 inches of pine straw or wood chips.

## Watering
- Do not let the soil dry out.
- Water when rainfall is less than normal, especially in hot weather.

## Fertilizing
- While the tree is young, feed it in March, May, and September with 1 cup of 10-10-10 fertilizer for each inch of trunk thickness measured 4 feet above the ground.

## Easy Tip
The more sun your dogwood gets, the more water it needs.

## Suggestions for Vigorous Growth
- Maintain mulch year-round.
- Leave lower limbs on trees to protect the trunk from cold and damage.

## Pest Control
- Most serious insects are borers, which often enter holes in trunks caused by lawn mowers or string trimmers.
- Flowering dogwood is subject to leaf spots during wet weather, and dogwood leaf blight is a serious disease that has killed many dogwoods along the East Coast—both can be controlled with fungicide, but keeping the tree well-watered in summer is the best way to prevent disease.

## Complementary Plants
- Try fothergilla (*Fothergilla gardenii*) or witchhazel (*Hamamelis* x *intermedia*) as dogwood companions.

## Recommended Selections
- 'Cherokee Chief' has deep-red flower bracts.
- 'Cloud 9' flowers profusely when young.
- 'Green Glow' has green leaves splotched with lighter green.

# Franklin Tree
*Franklinia alatamaha*

## A Beautiful Native Georgian Now Extinct in the Wild

First discovered in 1765 growing along the banks of the Altamaha River in southeastern Georgia by the great plant explorer John Bartram, the Franklinia was never again seen in the wild after 1803. Bartram named the lovely small tree after his friend Benjamin Franklin. A challenge to grow, the Franklin tree is well worth trying—it has beautiful, fragrant white flowers from mid-summer into fall, followed by beautiful orange and red fall leaves, sometimes accompanied by a late flower or two.

## Top Reasons to Plant

○ Beautiful large, showy late-summer blooms
○ Fragrant flowers
○ Spectacular fall color
○ Attractive form
○ Aristocratic history

## Useful Hint

It's believed that a disease associated with cotton also affects the Franklin tree, so don't plant it where cotton has been grown.

## Bloom Color
Creamy-white with bright-yellow stamens

## Bloom Period
Mid- to late summer until frost

## Height/Width
10 to 25 feet x 6 to 15 feet

## Planting Location
- Moist, acidic soil with lots of organic matter and excellent drainage
- Sun to partial shade (about a half-day of sun)
- Protected from strong winds

## Planting
- Plant small container-grown or balled-and-burlapped plants in midautumn or early spring.
- Dig the hole three to five times as wide as and the same depth as the rootball.
- If the soil is not naturally full of humus, add compost, planting mix, or other organic matter to achieve a 50-50 mix with original soil.
- Add 1 tablespoon of 0-46-0 fertilizer per foot of hole diameter.
- Set the plant in the hole and remove any burlap, twine, or wire.
- Water with a transplant solution.
- Fill the hole with soil dug from the hole.
- Water well.
- Mulch with 2 inches of pine straw over the entire root area.

## Watering
- Provide an inch of water in weeks without that amount of rainfall.
- Water regularly spring through fall.

*Easy Tip*

Though Franklin tree needs regular moisture throughout the growing season, it does not survive in constantly wet soil.

## Fertilizing
- No fertilizer is required.

## Suggestions for Vigorous Growth
- Grow the tree in well-drained, acidic soil.
- Provide regular water if rain is lacking.
- Keep lightly mulched year-round.

## Pest Control
- No serious pests or diseases trouble this tree, but wet soils will likely cause root rot.

## Complementary Plants
- This tree makes an outstanding specimen tree in a prominent place in the landscape.
- Combine with rhododendron and azalea.

## Recommended Selections
- There are no known cultivars, so plant the species.

# Fringe Tree
## *Chionanthus virginicus*

## A Beautiful Flowering Tree That Extends the Spring Season

The fringe tree's white flowers are held in masses just beyond its leaves, with the petals hanging from tiny, threadlike stems. The contrast of the white flowers against the new, vibrant green leaves is striking. When a slight breeze blows, the whole tree shakes, looking almost like a disco mirror ball in your spring landscape. The flowers are also fragrant, with some trees having a stronger perfume than others.

## Top Reasons to Plant

- Showy blooms in late spring to early summer
- Berries in late summer that attract birds
- Compact size
- Adapts to a variety of soils
- Tolerates pollution and other urban conditions
- Fragrant flowers

## Bloom Color
White blooms followed by bluish berries

## Bloom Period
Late spring to early summer

## Height/Width
10 to 15 feet x 8 to 10 feet

## Planting Location
- Best in moist, well-drained, acidic soil containing some organic matter
- Prefers full sun but will take light shade

## Planting
- Plant in midautumn or early spring.
- Dig the hole three to five times as wide as and as deep as the rootball.
- Add 1 cup of lime and 1 tablespoon of 0-46-0 fertilizer per foot of hole diameter.
- Place the tree in the hole and cut away any burlap, twine, or wire.
- Fill with dirt dug from the hole.
- Water well.
- Mulch with 2 inches of pine straw or wood chips.

## Watering
- Water heavily in weeks when temperatures rise above 95 degrees Fahrenheit.

## Fertilizing
- Spread compost or rotted leaves around the base of the tree each fall to feed it lightly.

## Easy Tip
Since fringe tree adapts well to urban life, it's good next to a patio or sidewalk—it's also beautiful near a water garden.

## Suggestions for Vigorous Growth
- Fringe tree leafs out late—don't worry if it doesn't have leaves yet when other trees do.
- To maintain tree shape, train to one main trunk—fringe tree is variable in its form, with some tending to be large bushes and others growing immediately into small trees.
- Prune immediately after flowering if pruning is needed.

## Pest Control
- Borers may be a problem, so keep lawn equipment from nicking holes in the trunk; such holes are entry points for borers.
- Scale—little brown "dots" on stems and beneath leaves—may appear but usually aren't a big problem.

## Complementary Plants
- Fringe tree goes well with late-spring and early-summer shrubs.

## Recommended Selections
- No cultivars are generally available.

## Useful Hint
Fringe tree produces bluish berries in August, which are much appreciated by a variety of birds.

# Ginkgo
*Ginkgo biloba*

## *An Ancient Tree with Fan-Shaped Leaves Turning Clear-Yellow in Autumn*

A view of the bright-yellow carpet of fall leaves under a gingko tree is a memory that can last a lifetime. Several huge ginkgos grow on the University of Georgia campus, where they've impressed visitors to football games for decades. The ginkgo's trunk grows vigorously for twenty years, usually producing small branches on all sides and a nice conical shape.

## Top Reasons to Plant

- Beautiful, unusual leaf shape
- Excellent yellow foliage in fall
- Majestic, ancient appearance
- Pest and disease resistant
- Outstanding shade tree

## *Useful Hint*

The ginkgo is one of our oldest trees—fossil records show it was native to North America and grew here one hundred fifty million years ago. It died out due to climate changes and was reintroduced to North America in 1784.

## Bloom Color
Insignificant green blooms

## Bloom Period
Midspring

## Height/Width
40 to 70 feet x 30 to 50 feet

## Planting Location
• Loose, well-drained soil, alkaline or acidic
• Sun

## Planting
• Buy named cultivars—which will be male; female trees develop awful-smelling, messy fruits.
• Plant in midautumn or early spring.
• Dig the hole three to five times as wide as and the same depth as the rootball.
• Add 1 cup of lime and 1 tablespoon of 0-46-0 fertilizer per foot of hole diameter.
• Place the tree in the hole and cut away all burlap, twine, or wire.
• Fill with dirt dug from the hole.
• Water thoroughly.
• Mulch with 2 inches of pine straw or wood chips.

## Watering
• Water frequently after transplanting.
• Once the tree is established, water deeply in weeks when summer temperatures rise above 95 degrees Fahrenheit.

## Fertilizing
• While the tree is young, feed it in March, May, and September with 1 cup of 10-10-10 fertilizer for each inch of trunk thickness measured 4 feet above the ground.

## Easy Tip
Be sure to buy nursery grown cultivars of ginkgos to guarantee you have a male—the females produce nasty-smelling, messy fruit to be avoided at all costs.

• Once the tree becomes established, little fertilizer is needed.

## Suggestions for Vigorous Growth
• If the young tree needs support, a stake placed 18 inches away from both sides of the trunk will keep it upright, but stake the tree so it can sway slightly.
• Prune at any time if needed.

## Pest Control
• No serious pests or diseases trouble this tree.

## Complementary Plants
• The shade cast by ginkgo isn't very dense, so you can underplant it with bulbs, ground covers, perennials, or shrubs.

## Recommended Selections
• 'Fastigiata' is more columnar than other ginkgos and is a good tree for lining a long driveway.
• 'Autumn Gold'™ is a symmetrical tree with excellent clear-yellow fall color.

# Golden Rain Tree
*Koelreuteria* species

## A Combination Shade and Flowering Tree with Gorgeous Yellow Blooms

Golden rain tree was introduced to the Americas from China before the Revolutionary War, though it was a late arrival to Georgia. The yellow flowers that cover the tree in June are quite unusual, as are the clusters of papery, lanternlike seed pods that follow the flowers. Golden rain tree is the perfect size for a suburban landscape. It grows relatively quickly, and its attractiveness makes it an excellent tree near pedestrian traffic.

## Top Reasons to Plant

- Showy clusters of yellow flowers in summer
- Decorative seedpods until fall
- Tolerates variety of soils and climates
- Permits grass to grow under it
- Good shade tree in summer
- Grows quickly
- Drought tolerant when established

## Useful Hint

Because golden rain tree has such deep roots, it's easy to grow grass around it.

## Bloom Color
Yellow

## Bloom Period
Summer

## Height/Width
20 to 40 feet x 20 to 30 feet

## Planting Location
- Adapts to any well-drained soil, whether acidic or alkaline
- Sun

## Planting
- Plant container-grown or balled-and-burlapped trees in midautumn or early spring.
- Dig the hole three to five times as wide as and as deep as the rootball.
- Add 1 cup of lime and 1 tablespoon of 0-46-0 fertilizer per foot of hole diameter.
- Place the tree in the hole, removing any burlap, wire, or twine.
- Fill with soil dug from the hole.
- Water thoroughly.
- Mulch with 2 inches of pine straw or wood chips.

## Watering
- Until the tree is established, water deeply when rainfall is less than an inch per week.
- Water heavily each week when the temperature rises above 95 degrees Fahrenheit.

## Fertilizing
- While the tree is young, feed it in March, May, and September with 1 cup of 10-10-10 fertilizer for each inch of

## *Easy Tip*

For attractive dried arrangements, harvest the pink seed capsules of bougainvillea golden rain tree when they're at their peak, then hang them to dry in a large plastic bag containing a pound of silica gel—this quick drying action will keep the color fresh.

trunk thickness measured 4 feet above the ground.

## Suggestions for Vigorous Growth
- For the first three years, remove the branch tips each March to force more limbs to sprout.

## Pest Control
- Few insects or diseases trouble this tree.

## Complementary Plants
- Plant with ornamental grasses such as maiden grass or fountain grass.

## Recommended Selections
- The common golden rain tree (*Koelreuteria paniculata*) has brown seed pods.
- Bougainvillea golden rain tree (*Koelreuteria bipinnata*) is a smaller tree with yellow flowers in late summer and early autumn; it features more colorful seed capsules.

51

# Japanese Cryptomeria

*Cryptomeria japonica*

*A Fast-Growing Needled Evergreen That Stands Up to Georgia Summers*

It's surprising that Japanese cryptomeria isn't more widely planted in Georgia—it's evergreen and makes a fine screen; it's tall and symmetrical, making it an impressive specimen tree; and it's more narrow than wide, so it can be placed near homes and buildings without fear of encroachment. Removing lower limbs reveals attractive, reddish brown bark.

## Top Reasons to Plant

- Tolerates summer heat and humidity
- Beautiful, graceful "needled" evergreen
- Adaptable to soils and sun
- Excellent specimen tree
- Dwarf forms available for smaller properties
- Disease and insect resistant

## Useful Hint

Japanese cryptomeria needs full sunshine—in shade it becomes thin and ragged.

## Bloom Color
Grown for its year-round foliage, dark-green in summer, sometimes purple or bronze in winter

## Bloom Period
Foliage effective year-round

## Height/Width
30 to 60 feet x 10 to 25 feet

## Planting Location
- Sheltered from strong winds
- Rich, moist, acidic, well-drained soil
- Sun
- Not suited for coastal Georgia

## Planting
- Plant in midautumn or early spring.
- Dig the hole three to five times as wide as and exactly as deep as the rootball.
- Add 1 cup of lime and 1 tablespoon of 0-46-0 fertilizer per foot of hole diameter.
- Place the tree in the hole and cut away any burlap, twine, or wire.
- Fill with dirt that came from hole.
- Water thoroughly.
- Mulch with 2 inches of pine straw or wood chips.

## Watering
- This tree needs ample moisture to perform at its best.
- Water when weekly rainfall doesn't total an inch.

## Fertilizing
- While the tree is young, feed it in March, May, and September with 1 cup of 10-10-10 fertilizer for each inch of trunk thickness measured 4 feet above the ground.

## Easy Tip
For small spaces, look into the dwarf cultivars of Japanese cryptomeria.

- Once the tree is mature, little fertilizer is needed.

## Suggestions for Vigorous Growth
- In early years, shear off half the length of the new green branch tips in May to encourage denser growth.

## Pest Control
- Bagworms can affect Japanese cryptomeria—look for 3-inch-long bags of needles hanging from branch tips in August; pick them off and destroy them.

## Complementary Plants
- Japanese cryptomeria makes a fine screen—plant two staggered rows with the trees 10 feet apart.
- This tree is ideal for Asian-inspired gardens.

## Recommended Selections
- One of the best cultivars for Georgia is 'Yoshino'—it is fast growing, has blue-green summer foliage, and grows strongly in a variety of situations.

# Japanese Maple

*Acer palmatum*

### A Beautiful Tree with Many Forms That Tolerates Shade

Thousands of years of cultivation and selection have resulted in the existence of literally hundreds of attractive Japanese maple cultivars. Leaf colors range from bright-red-purple to deep-green. Leaves have broad, rounded lobes or a finely divided, almost ferny, character. Japanese maples can produce wonderful fall leaf colors, but colors may not be as bright in the warmer parts of Georgia.

## Top Reasons to Plant

- Stunning small trees
- Beautiful spring, summer, and fall colors
- Intriguing branch structure
- Elegant choice for shady gardens
- Excellent near water gardens
- Insect and disease resistant

## Useful Hint

The foliage shape of Japanese maples can be chosen to blend or contrast with surrounding plantings.

## Bloom Color
Insignificant purple blooms

## Bloom Period
Late spring

## Height/Width
2 to 20 feet x 4 to 20 feet

## Planting Location
- Moist, well-drained soil containing organic matter
- Partial shade—dappled shade beneath tall trees is ideal
- Protected from winds—the east or north side of a home is usually excellent

## Planting
- Plant in fall just after the weather has begun to turn cool.
- Dig the hole three times as wide as and as deep as the rootball.
- Water with transplanting solution.
- Fill with soil dug from the hole.
- Mulch with 1 to 2 inches of pine straw or wood chips.

## Watering
- Never let this tree dry out.
- It is especially important to keep the soil moist when the plant is young and during droughts.
- If the edges of leaves turn first yellow, then brown and dry, the tree is not receiving adequate water.

## Fertilizing
- Feed once in April with 1 tablespoon of 10-10-10 fertilizer for every foot of plant height.

## *Easy Tip*
If you plant a Japanese maple in spring, be prepared to provide it with plenty of water over the summer—a July drought will almost certainly result in scorched leaves.

## Suggestions for Vigorous Growth
- Maintain mulch year-round.
- Do not prune off lower limbs—they add grace and charm to the tree.
- In January, remove or shorten any long, vigorous sprouts back to side branches.

## Pest Control
- Few pests bother this tree.

## Complementary Plants
- Japanese maple makes an elegant focal point for partially shaded yards.
- Cascading types add appeal near water gardens.

## Recommended Selections
- 'Bloodgood' is crimson in spring and darkens to deep-red in summer.
- 'Atropurpureum' has wonderful red leaves in spring, which usually fade to dark-green in summer.
- 'Beni Hime' has miniature leaves and a twiggy branch structure.
- Any of the smaller "Dissectum" varieties with their finely divided leaves make a nice texture variation in the landscape.

# Japanese Snowbell
*Styrax japonicus*

## A Charming Little Tree with Year-Round Appeal

One of the last flowers to bloom in spring is the beautiful Japanese snowbell. The blossoms are clusters of drooping, yellow-centered, bell-shaped, white flowers with a faint perfume. The leaves are glossy, a rich green in summer and yellow or red in fall. They perch on the topside of the branches, making the flowers easy to see. Green-white, egg-shaped fruits follow the flowers. A charming little tree, the Japanese snowbell has a spreading crown that casts light shade.

## Top Reasons to Plant

○ Lovely, late-spring flowers
○ Fragrant blossoms
○ Nice fall color
○ Interesting winter structure and bark
○ Attracts butterflies
○ Few pests and diseases

## Useful Hint

Japanese snowbell is especially effective near a patio or on a hillside where you can look up into the flower display.

## Bloom Color
White

## Bloom Period
Late spring

## Height/Width
15 to 30 feet x 15 to 30 feet

## Planting Location
- Moist, acidic, well-drained soil with lots of organic matter
- Sun or partial shade

## Planting
- Plant in early spring.
- Dig the hole the same depth as the rootball and three to five times as wide.
- Add 1 cup of lime and 1 tablespoon of 0-46-0 fertilizer per foot of hole diameter.
- Set the tree so the top of the rootball is about an inch above ground level.
- Cut away any burlap, twine, or wire.
- Fill the hole with soil.
- Water thoroughly.
- Mulch with 2 inches of pine straw or wood chips.

## Watering
- Water well in weeks without an inch of rainfall, especially if temperatures are above 95 degrees Fahrenheit.

## Fertilizing
- While the tree is young, feed it in March, May, and September with 1 cup of 10-10-10 fertilizer for each inch of trunk thickness measured 4 feet above the ground.

## Easy Tip
The smooth gray-brown bark of Japanese snowbell adds texture to the garden in winter.

- Once the tree matures, little fertilizer is needed.

## Suggestions for Vigorous Growth
- If a young tree needs support, place a stake 18 inches from either side of the trunk, and attach the tree loosely enough that it can sway slightly.
- Keep mulched year-round.
- Prune to control shape—this tree may take on a shrubby form.

## Pest Control
- Few pests and diseases trouble this tree.

## Complementary Plants
- Plant on the edge of an open woodland with azalea, mountain laurel, and rhododendron.

## Recommended Selections
- 'Pendula' is a graceful, weeping cultivar.
- 'Pink Chimes' has a shrubby form and pink flowers.

# Japanese Stewartia

*Stewartia pseudocamellia*

## A Beautiful Small Tree with Lots of Assets

Stewartias bear 2$^{1}/_{2}$- to 3$^{1}/_{2}$-inch, camellia-like flowers in mid- to late summer. They not only have exquisite creamy-white flowers but also display colorful fall foliage and peeling bark that shows cinnamon, red, gray, and shades of orange. Purple-bronze leaves emerge in early spring. In summer, the leaves turn green; come cold weather, they change to yellow, purple-orange, and bronze-red. As the plant matures, the bark peels to expose striking patterns of color.

## Top Reasons to Plant

- Gorgeous, camellia-like blooms
- Beautiful fall color
- Interesting, colorful winter bark
- Pest and disease resistant
- Flowers in late summer
- Excellent small tree

## Useful Hint

It's not unusual for Japanese stewartia to take three to five years to become a fully established, full-blooming plant, but it's definitely worth the wait.

## Bloom Color
Creamy-white petals with orange anthers

## Bloom Period
Mid- to late summer

## Height/Width
30 to 40 feet x 20 to 30 feet

## Planting Location
• Fertile, moist, acidic soil containing lots of organic matter
• Sun is best for flowers and fall color; afternoon shade is appreciated.

## Planting
• Plant small, young, container-grown or balled-and-burlapped trees in early spring while they are still dormant.
• Dig the hole three times as wide as and twice as deep as the rootball.
• Set the plant in the hole so the crown (where trunk and roots meet) is an inch above ground level.
• Fill with dirt dug from the hole.
• Shape the earth around the crown into a wide saucer.
• Water slowly and deeply.
• Apply mulch 3 inches deep and 3 inches away from the trunk.

## Watering
• During the first year, in weeks without an inch of rain, water deeply every two weeks during spring and fall, and every seven to ten days in summer.

## Easy Tip
Japanese stewartia does well only in the cooler parts of Georgia—silky stewartia (*Stewartia malacodendron*) is a southeastern native that will take the heat in the warmer areas of the state.

## Fertilizing
• Apply slow-release, acidic fertilizer in late winter or early spring.
• Water fertilizer in well.

## Suggestions for Vigorous Growth
• Maintain mulch year-round.

## Pest Control
• No serious pests or diseases bother this tree.

## Complementary Plants
• Japanese stewartia makes a beautiful lawn specimen.
• Group in a shrub border with low-growing azaleas.

## Recommended Selections
• Korean stewartia (*Stewartia koreana*) may be a better fit for small gardens, growing to 20 to 30 feet, but is otherwise similar to Japanese stewartia.
• Chinese stewartia (*Stewartia sinensis*) is smaller still, reaching 15 to 25 feet, with otherwise similar attributes.

59

# Japanese Zelkova

*Zelkova serrata*

## A Fast-Growing Shade Tree Reminiscent of the Elm

We Americans are impatient. When we plant a tree, we want it to be big as soon as possible. So when we buy a tree, the first (and sometimes only) question we ask is, "How quickly does it grow?" That leads to many bad choices because fast-growing trees usually develop problems you want to avoid. That's *not* true of Japanese zelkova, which may grow several feet a year when young. It's a well-mannered tree with foliage similar to the elm and with interesting bark.

## Top Reasons to Plant

- Fast growing but strong
- Interesting winter bark
- Excellent substitute for the elm
- Pollution resistant
- Few pests and disease
- Outstanding shade tree
- Drought tolerant when established

## Useful Hint

The bark on a Japanese zelkova is reddish when the tree is young, changing to gray and mottled on mature specimens.

## Bloom Color
Insignificant blooms

## Bloom Period
Spring

## Height/Width
50 to 90 feet x 40 to 60 feet

## Planting Location
- Moist, well-drained soil, either acidic or alkaline
- Sun

## Planting
- Plant from spring through fall.
- Dig the hole twice as wide as and as deep as the rootball.
- Place the tree in the hole, removing any synthetic burlap or twine.
- Water well with transplanting solution.
- Using soil dug from the hole, pack the soil around the tree's roots.
- Mulch lightly with pine straw, shredded leaves, or fine pine bark.

## Watering
- Water deeply but regularly in the early years.
- Once established, this tree's deep root system helps it tolerate drought.

## Fertilizing
- This tree grows well without fertilizer.
- If a late frost kills young leaves, fertilize in late fall with a high-nitrogen tree fertilizer spread in a circle around the tree's base according to package directions.
- Water fertilizer in well.

# Easy Tip

This pollution-resistant tree is a good choice for urban areas or near highways.

## Suggestions for Vigorous Growth
- Spring frosts may damage the leaves of young trees, but the leaves grow back.
- Prune in winter as needed, removing any crowded branches.

## Pest Control
- This tree occasionally suffers from disease or insects, especially beetles, but the problem is usually not serious.

## Complementary Plants
- Japanese zelkova makes an ideal shade tree.

## Recommended Selections
- 'Green Vase'® grows especially quickly and has more consistent fall color than many zelkovas.

# Katsura Tree
*Cercidiphyllum japonicum*

## A Beautiful, Refined Shade Tree Planted for Its Foliage

Katsura is a beautiful, fast- to medium-fast-growing, refined shade tree with outstanding foliage. The new leaves in spring are a bronze or reddish purple, changing to blue-green in summer, then transforming in fall to a spectacular, glowing, apricot-orange and golden-yellow—a sight worth traveling to see. The aging leaves give off a faint, spicy scent. The tree has a dense rounded form and shaggy brown bark that adds interest to the winter landscape.

## Top Reasons to Plant

- Beautiful leaves shaped like those of a redbud
- Fast growing
- Spectacular fall foliage
- Shaggy brown bark interesting in winter
- Fragrant leaves
- Few pests and diseases
- Outstanding shade tree for medium-sized landscapes

## Useful Hint

The noted plantsman and author Michael Dirr of the University of Georgia says, "If I could use only one tree, this would be my first tree."

## Bloom Color

Grown for its leaves, which emerge bronze or reddish purple, change to bluish green in summer, then turn apricot-orange and gold in fall

## Bloom Period

Foliage effective spring through fall

## Height/Width

40 to 50 feet x 20 to 30 feet

## Planting Location

- Well-drained, moist, acidic soil with lots of organic matter
- Sun

## Planting

- Choose a *young*, dormant, container-grown or balled-and-burlapped tree—this tree does not easily transplant successfully.
- Plant in early spring.
- Dig the hole three times the width of the rootball and twice as deep.
- Set the tree in the hole so the crown (where trunk and roots meet) is an inch or so above ground level.
- Fill in with soil dug from the hole.
- With remaining soil, make a wide saucer around the tree.
- Water slowly and deeply.
- Apply 3 inches of mulch starting 3 inches from the trunk.

## Watering

- In the first year, unless a soaking rain falls each week, water deeply every two weeks in spring and fall, and every seven to ten days in summer.

*Easy Tip*

Be sure to buy a single-stemmed plant to ensure a strong, straight trunk.

- For the first two or three years, water deeply when your flowers need watering.

## Fertilizing

- Apply complete slow-release fertilizer in late winter.
- Water fertilizer in well.

## Suggestions for Vigorous Growth

- Maintain mulch year-round.
- Prune in late winter to feature the main stem and to create a broad crown.

## Pest Control

- No serious pests or diseases trouble this tree.

## Complementary Plants

- Katsura is best used as a specimen tree where it can be seen year-round.

## Recommended Selections

- The species is highly recommended.
- The weeping form, 'Pendula', is a lovely small tree that grows to 15 to 25 feet tall.

# Korean Dogwood

*Cornus kousa*

## An Excellent Substitute for the Native Flowering Dogwood

Gardeners do a double-take when they see a dogwood still in bloom in May or even June. It's the Korean dogwood, a tree that blooms weeks later than the native flowering dogwood. And the Korean dogwood comes into its glory after its leaves have emerged. The leaves are more slender than those of the flowering dogwood and appear to be a deeper green. In fall, seeds appear in tight clusters, resembling a red raspberry rising above the branch tip.

## Top Reasons to Plant

- Beautiful white flowers in late spring through early summer
- Showy red fruits in late summer
- Reddish purple or scarlet leaves in fall
- Resists anthracnose disease, which affects native dogwoods
- Tolerates more sun than flowering dogwoods
- Horizontal branching habit attractive in winter
- Interesting bark in winter

## Bloom Color
White

## Bloom Period
Late spring through early summer

## Height/Width
10 to 20 feet x 10 to 20 feet

## Planting Location
- Well-drained, acidic soil with lots of organic matter
- Sun but with afternoon shade

## Planting
- Plant in midautumn or early spring.
- Dig the hole three to five times as wide as and the same depth as the rootball.
- Add 1 tablespoon of 0-46-0 fertilizer per foot of hole diameter.
- Place the tree in the hole and cut away all burlap, wire, and twine.
- Fill with soil dug from the hole.
- Water thoroughly.
- Spread a 2-inch layer of pine straw or wood chips over the planting area.

## Watering
- Water well until established.
- If summer temperatures go above 95 degrees Fahrenheit, water heavily each week even if the tree is established.

*Easy Tip*

Keep a wide band of mulch around the trunk so mowers and string trimmers can't come close enough to create wounds through which borers can enter.

## Fertilizing
- In March, May, and September, apply 1 cup of 10-10-10 fertilizer for each inch of thickness of trunk 4 feet above ground.

## Suggestions for Vigorous Growth
- Light pruning may be done anytime if needed.
- Keep mulch in place year-round.

## Pest Control
- Kousa dogwood resists borers and anthracnose disease.

## Complementary Plants
- Plant with spring- and early-summer-flowering shrubs and perennials.

## Recommended Selections
- The flowers of 'Moonbeam' may reach 8 inches wide.
- *Cornus kousa* var. *chinensis* 'Milky Way', a form of kousa dogwood, has numerous flowers and a bushy form nice for smaller landscapes.

*Useful Hint*

Kousa dogwood resists the anthracnose disease *Discula distructiva* that has killed so many flowering dogwoods in the South and East, and it seems to resist dogwood borer, as well.

# Kwanzan Cherry

*Prunus serrulata* 'Kwanzan'

*A Beautiful Spring-Flowering Cherry with Double Pink Blooms*

Thanks to cherry-blossom festivals, flowering cherries are gaining attention and becoming an increasing presence in the spring landscape. The Kwanzan cherry is one of the best, known for large, double, rosy-pink flowers in April and leaves that are reddish when new and bronze in fall. This free-flowering variety offers a spectacular blooming display in spring.

## Top Reasons to Plant

- Beautiful spring show of blooms
- Attractive bark
- Relatively small stature
- Good cut flower
- Fragrant blooms
- Nice fall color

## Useful Hint

It seems inelegant to say anything negative about such a beautiful show, but fallen blooms should be cleaned immediately from the deck or patio—they're quite slippery.

## Bloom Color
Deep pink

## Bloom Period
Spring

## Height/Width
15 to 20 feet x 15 to 25 feet

## Planting Location
• Fast-draining soil that contains organic matter
• Full sun

## Planting
• Plant in spring or early autumn.
• In clay soils, consider planting Kwanzan cherry on a mound or in a raised bed to avoid the possibility of root rot.
• Dig the hole as deep as the rootball and twice as wide.
• Place the tree in the hole and water with transplanting solution.
• Fill in around roots with soil from the hole.
• Water well.
• Mulch lightly.

## Watering
• Water when rainfall measures less than an inch per week.
• Be careful not to overwater in clay soil.

## Fertilizing
• Fertilize in late fall with a high-nitrogen fertilizer for trees, following label directions.

## Easy Tip
Cut branches of flowering cherry while in bloom to use in arrangements.

## Suggestions for Vigorous Growth
• Prune as necessary after flowers fade.
• Maintain light mulch to prevent trunk damage from lawn equipment.

## Pest Control
• Insects and diseases are often troublesome—affected trees tend not to be long-lived.
• Bacterial canker and bot canker, appearing as oozing areas on the bark, may occur.
• Consult the Extension Service for causes and cures for any problems that arise.

## Complementary Plants
• Underplant with spring-flowering bulbs in companionable colors.

## Recommended Selections
• 'Amanogawa' is quite columnar, about 20 feet tall and only 5 feet wide.
• 'Royal Burgundy' has deep-pink flowers and a lovely mahogany-red trunk.

# Leyland Cypress

*Cupressaceae × cupressocyparis leylandii*

*A Fast-Growing Evergreen for Screens and Hedges*

Leyland cypress is one of the most attractive fast-growing screen plants in Georgia. Its bluish green foliage grows densely from near ground level up to its tip. The tree is strongly columnar—even at a height of 40 feet, it will be only 8 feet wide at its base. Our growing conditions produce large Leyland cypress trees. These same growing conditions make Leyland cypress susceptible to a disease called bot canker against which there is little defense.

## Top Reasons to Plant

○ Fast-growing evergreen
○ Useful for screening or tall hedge
○ Feathery, bluish green foliage
○ Attractive, scaly red-brown bark
○ Tolerates heavy shearing or pruning

## Useful Hint

Leyland cypress grows up to 3 feet per year, so it reaches 60 to 70 feet very quickly for an evergreen.

## Bloom Color
Grown for its soft, blue-green foliage

## Bloom Period
Foliage effective year-round

## Height/Width
8 to 40 feet x 4 to 8 feet

## Planting Location
- Well-drained, fertile soil with organic matter so it holds moisture
- Sun or partial shade

## Planting
- Plant in spring or fall.
- Dig the hole at least 5 feet wide and 1 foot deep even for just a 1-gallon plant.
- If planting a hedge, make the planting bed 5 feet wide and space plants 3 to 5 feet apart.
- Thoroughly break up the soil in the hole, as well as the soil taken from it.
- Place the tree in the hole and fill with soil.
- Water thoroughly.
- Mulch 1 to 3 inches deep—but mulch should not touch the trunk.

## Watering
- Water regularly, especially the first year.
- Do not let roots dry out in summer heat.

## Fertilizing
- To increase the growth rate, apply 1 tablespoon of 10-10-10 fertilizer for each foot of plant height in March, June, and August until the tree reaches the desired height.

## Easy Tip
Nothing beats Leyland cypress for fast growth as an evergreen screen or hedge, but it requires pruning and a good bit of room, and is susceptible to several diseases—so consider your options carefully.

## Suggestions for Vigorous Growth
- Stake plants 5 feet tall or less.
- Top or prune in late winter or in spring—Leyland cypress can be pruned to any height.
- Do not remove more than one-third of the foliage in any one season.

## Pest Control
- This tree is subject to bot canker, with branches turning bright-rust.
- There's no chemical control for bot canker, so remove affected limbs or entire trees.
- Remove any bagworms that appear as they can threaten the life of the tree.

## Complementary Plants
- Use as an evergreen backdrop for flowering trees and shrubs.

## Recommended Selections
- 'Haggerston Gray' has green foliage with a slightly gray cast.
- 'Castlewellan Gold'® has golden-yellow foliage.

# Oak

*Quercus* species

## Majestic Native Trees with a Lot of Variety

Dozens of oaks grow well in Georgia. At about 40 feet tall, sawtooth oak (*Quercus acutissima*) is one of the smaller oaks. Shumard oak (*Q. shumardii*) and scarlet oak (*Q. coccinea*) are two of the best oaks for red fall color. Red oak (*Q. rubra*) is easy to transplant and grows rapidly into a large tree. Live oak (*Q. virginiana*) is the Georgia state tree—it's best suited for the southern half of the state.

## Top Reasons to Plant

○ Beautiful, majestic shade trees
○ Good fall color
○ Generally fast growing
○ Few pests and diseases
○ Adaptable to varying soils
○ Drought tolerant when established

## Useful Hint

Before you plant an oak, think about its space needs—check on all sides for sun-loving plants the oak might shade, and look overhead for telephone and electrical lines.

## Bloom Color
Grown for the foliage

## Bloom Period
Foliage effective spring through fall

## Height/Width
40 to 80 feet x 50 to 90 feet

## Planting Location
- Prefers slightly acidic, sandy loam soils, but tolerates moist clay and dry areas
- Sun

## Planting
- Plant in midautumn or early spring.
- Dig the hole three to five times as wide as and as deep as the rootball.
- Add 1 cup of lime and 1 tablespoon of 0-46-0 fertilizer per foot of hole diameter.
- Place the tree in the hole and cut away all burlap, twine, or wire.
- Fill the hole with soil and water thoroughly.
- Mulch with 2 inches of pine straw or wood chips.

## Watering
- Water regularly during the first season.
- Once the tree is established, water heavily each week if temperatures rise above 95 degrees Fahrenheit.

## Fertilizing
- While the tree is young, feed it in March, May, and September with 1 cup of 10-10-10 fertilizer for each inch of trunk thickness measured 4 feet above the ground.
- Once the tree matures, little fertilizer is needed.

# Easy Tip
Keep in mind that it's difficult to grow grass in the shade of a mature oak tree.

## Suggestions for Vigorous Growth
- If a young tree needs support, place a stake 18 inches away from both sides of the trunk, and stake the tree loosely enough that it can sway slightly.
- The major cause of death for mature oaks is construction damage—if you're building on a wooded lot, tell your builder which trees must be protected, and ensure no machinery comes closer than the dripline (the area extending to the edges of the branch ends).

## Pest Control
- Few pests and diseases bother this tree.

## Complementary Plants
- Oaks are majestic specimen trees, and when mature, they cast shade that's much loved by many shrubs, such as azalea and rhododendron.

## Recommended Selections
- The water oak (*Quercus nigra*) grows in a wide variety of soil types and tolerates wet or dry sites—it has little fall color, but grows very fast and makes a fine shade tree.

# Ornamental Pear

*Pyrus calleryana*

### A Showy Spring Bloomer with Better Choices Than 'Bradford'

Most people refer to this tree as "Bradford pear." That's the name of the first and most commonly planted cultivar, but many other cultivars have the characteristic white flowers early in spring, glossy green leaves in summer, and excellent fall foliage color. *All* are better than 'Bradford', which has what experts call narrow crotch angles, which often cause limbs to break and the tree to split in half.

## Top Reasons to Plant

- White flowers in early spring
- Glossy green leaves in summer
- Beautiful fall color
- Good for screening
- Tolerates dry soil when established
- Few insect problems

## Useful Hint

Avoid planting the 'Bradford' cultivar, which has lots of structural problems—instead, choose another variety of ornamental pear.

## Bloom Color
White

## Bloom Period
Early spring

## Height/Width
30 to 50 feet x 16 to 35 feet

## Planting Location
- Tolerates many types of soil as long as it's well-drained
- Sun

## Planting
- Plant in late winter or early spring.
- Dig the hole as deep as the rootball and three to five times as wide.
- Place the tree in the hole and remove any burlap, wire, or twine.
- Pack soil from the hole around the rootball.
- Water thoroughly.
- Mulch lightly with 2 inches of pine straw or wood chips.

## Watering
- When the tree is young, water deeply when there's been less than an inch of rain in a week.

## Fertilizing
- No fertilizer is needed.

## Easy Tip

Ornamental pears grow to be very large trees—space and site them according to their mature height and spread.

## Suggestions for Vigorous Growth
- Prune as needed in late winter.

## Pest Control
- Insects are rarely a problem.
- Fireblight may occur, causing leaves and stems to appear as if boiling water had been poured over them— immediately prune back to nondiseased wood, disinfecting the saw or pruners between cuts.

## Complementary Plants
- This tree has a stiff, formal appearance that looks out of place in informal or naturalistic landscapes, so put it in a more formal, stylized setting.

## Recommended Selections
- 'Chanticleer'® isn't as large a tree as 'Bradford'.
- 'Edgewood' has silvery-green foliage.
- 'Fauriei' has a pyramidal shape.
- Good for small yards, 'Korean Sun'® grows about 12 feet tall and 15 feet wide.

# Paperbark Maple

*Acer griseum*

### A Beautiful Four-Season Tree That Fits Most Yards

Paperbark maple is perhaps the most beautiful of the three Georgia trees appreciated for their peeling bark (the other two are river birch and crapemyrtle). The young trunk and stems of a paperbark maple are a rich reddish brown. As the trunk and major limbs age, the bark becomes lighter and begins peeling back. The gray-red of the thin sheets of peeling bark contrasts wonderfully with the polished cinnamon-red wood beneath.

## Top Reasons to Plant

○ Beautiful, reddish brown, peeling bark
○ Outstanding fall foliage
○ Interesting seedpods
○ No serious pests or diseases
○ Needs little maintenance
○ Excellent near windows where its winter bark can be admired
○ Suitable for small yards

## Useful Hint

This tree makes a good focal point for a small yard or along the sunny edge of the woods on a larger property.

## Bloom Color
Inconspicuous blooms

## Bloom Period
Spring

## Height/Width
15 to 30 feet x 10 to 20 feet

## Planting Location
- Prefers moist, well-drained soil but is adaptable
- Sun

## Planting
- Plant in fall or spring.
- Dig the hole three to five times as wide as the rootball and as deep.
- Add 1 cup of lime and 1 tablespoon of 0-46-0 fertilizer per foot of hole diameter.
- Place the tree in the hole and cut away all burlap, twine, or wire.
- Fill with soil dug from the hole.
- Water thoroughly.
- Mulch with 2 inches of pine straw or wood chips.

## Watering
- Don't let the soil dry out.
- Water regularly if the soil isn't naturally moist and rainfall is lacking.
- Once the tree becomes established, water heavily each week if temperatures rise above 95 degrees Fahrenheit.

## Fertilizing
- This tree grows slowly (less than 1 foot per year) unless fertilized.

## Easy Tip
If you've been looking for something wonderfully different in a tree, paperbark maple is it.

- While the tree is young, feed it in March, May, and September with 1 cup of 10-10-10 fertilizer for each inch of trunk thickness measured 4 feet above the ground.

## Suggestions for Vigorous Growth
- If pruning is required, do it in winter.
- Maintain year-round mulch to keep moisture in the soil.

## Pest Control
- No serious pest problems trouble this tree.

## Complementary Plants
- Paperbark maple shows off its bark in winter if planted in a bermudagrass lawn that turns light brown when dormant—the same effect can be achieved by planting maiden grass (*Miscanthus sinensis*) nearby.

## Recommended Selections
- Few cultivars are available yet, but 'Gingerbread'™ ('Ginzam') and 'Cinnamon Flake' are both excellent.

# Persian Ironwood

*Parrotia persica*

### A Choice Small Tree That's Attractive All Year

This witchhazel relative is a beauty in every season. It has unusual blooms before it leafs out—closely packed red stamens surrounded by a woolly brown bract—giving the overall tree a crimson glow. The leaves emerge reddish purple, then change to lustrous dark-green for summer, but the real show begins in fall. Persian ironwood's leaves first turn golden-yellow, then pinkish orange, and finally scarlet.

## Top Reasons to Plant

○ Stunning fall foliage
○ Small scale makes it suitable for most yards
○ Beautiful scaling bark provides winter interest
○ Pest and disease free
○ Picturesque branching structure
○ Drought resistant when established

## Useful Hint

Depending on the seed source, Persian ironwood can grow as a multistemmed large shrub or a more upright tree—some pruning is needed in its youth to give it the form you prefer.

## Bloom Color
Reddish brown

## Bloom Period
Late winter through early spring

## Height/Width
20 to 40 feet x 15 to 30 feet

## Planting Location
- Average, well-drained soil—it won't tolerate standing water
- Sun or light shade

## Planting
- Plant balled-and-burlapped trees in early spring.
- Dig the hole three to five times as wide as and as deep as the rootball.
- Place the tree in the hole and fill with soil from the hole.
- Water well.
- Mulch with 2 inches of shredded bark, fine bark, or pine straw.

## Watering
- Water well the first few seasons, watering deeply in weeks with less than an inch of rain.
- Though drought tolerant once established, this tree appreciates occasional watering during dry spells.

## *Easy Tip*
Persian ironwood becomes dramatic in the winter garden once it reaches the age that its bark begins peeling.

## Fertilizing
- No fertilizer is needed.

## Suggestions for Vigorous Growth
- Prune in spring in the early years to create a graceful shape.

## Pest Control
- This tree is pest and disease free.

## Complementary Plants
- For a dramatic fall display, plant Persian ironwood with other members of the witchhazel family—witchhazel, fothergilla, and winter hazel.
- Underplant with hellebore and epimedium.

## Recommended Selections
- 'Pendula' is a weeping form.

# Pine

*Pinus* species

## A Valued Tall Evergreen with Several Choices

Pine trees grow in all parts of Georgia. Loblolly pine (*Pinus taeda*) is often called Georgia pine because it's so common across the state. It grows tall very quickly, but after a few years, its foliage is too far above the ground to provide much screening. White pine (*P. strobus*) has soft, green-gray needles, and grows 60 feet tall with branches symmetrically whorled around its trunk. Virginia pine (*P. virginiana*) makes a dense, dark-green screen only 30 feet tall.

## Top Reasons to Plant

○ Evergreen needles
○ Grows quickly
○ Adapts to varying soils
○ Requires little care
○ Good for screening

## Useful Hint

White pine and Virginia pine form the best screens—if you have room, plant them in two staggered rows with 10 feet between plants. Some can be removed later when they become crowded.

## Bloom Color
Grown for its evergreen needles

## Bloom Period
Foliage effective year-round

## Height/Width
15 to 90 feet by 10 to 25 feet

## Planting Location
• Prefers fertile, well-drained soil but adapts to a variety of conditions
• Sun

## Planting
• Plant in fall or early spring.
• Dig the hole three times as wide as and as deep as the rootball.
• Add 1 cup of lime and 1 tablespoon of 0-46-0 fertilizer per foot of hole diameter.
• Place the tree in the hole and cut away all burlap, twine, or wire.
• Fill the hole with soil and water thoroughly.
• Mulch with 2 inches of pine straw or wood chips.

## Watering
• Water regularly until the tree becomes established.
• Once the tree is established, water heavily each week if temperatures rise above 95 degrees Fahrenheit.

## Fertilizing
• While the tree is young, feed it in March, May, and September with 1 cup of 10-10-10 fertilizer for each inch of trunk thickness measured 4 feet above the ground.
• Once the tree is mature, little fertilizer is needed.

# *Easy Tip*

Hardwood trees planted near pines eventually catch up with the pines and kill them with their shade.

## Suggestions for Vigorous Growth
• Shear for shape in May when new growth at the ends of branches is 3 inches long—cut all these "candles" in half, forcing them to resprout to create denser foliage.

## Pest Control
• Numerous pests and diseases may attack pines, but healthy trees can usually cope with them.

## Complementary Plants
• Pines are excellent to provide shade for woodland gardens and for shrubs preferring partial shade.

## Recommended Selections
• Loblolly pines grow well throughout the state.
• Plant white pines and Virginia pines only in the northern half of the state—they're subject to decline from heat and drought.

# Purple Leaf Plum
*Prunus cerasifera*

## A Lovely Small Tree with Pink Blossoms and Purple Leaves

Purple leaf plum puts on a striking show all summer with its dark-purple-red leaves, which may attract a good bit of attention from passersby. The tree blooms in early spring with small, showy white or pink blossoms covering it entirely. It's a relatively small tree that fits well into urban yards and gardens. If you're looking for spring to fall color for your yard, take a look at the purple leaf plum.

## Top Reasons to Plant

○ Beautiful spring blossoms
○ Richly colored leaves all summer and fall
○ Small scale fits into most settings
○ Adds good color around patios, decks, and gazebos
○ Can be used in large containers or planters

## Useful Hint

Small branches of purple leaf plum can be cut in late winter and taken indoors to bloom in a vase in a sunny, warm spot.

## Bloom Color
White, pink, or purple

## Bloom Period
Spring

## Height/Width
15 to 25 feet x 10 to 20 feet

## Planting Location
- Moist, well-drained, fertile soil
- Sun

## Planting
- Plant container-grown or balled-and-burlapped trees in spring.
- Dig the hole three times as wide as and as deep as the rootball.
- Set the tree in the hole and remove any burlap, twine, or wire.
- Fill with soil from the hole.
- Water well.
- Mulch with 2 inches of pine straw or wood chips.

## Watering
- Water as needed to prevent the soil from drying out.

## Fertilizing
- Feed with a long-lasting, slow-release fertilizer four times annually—as new growth begins, ten weeks later, again ten weeks after that, and once in fall.

## Suggestions for Vigorous Growth
- Prune to shape in early spring.
- Remove dead branches and twigs anytime.

### Easy Tip
Purple leaves make a real statement in the landscape, so make sure they mix comfortably with the other colors in your yard.

## Pest Control
- Fireblight and root rot may be problems—consult the Extension Service for controls.
- Peach tree borers may attack unhealthy trees, so keep yours healthy.

## Complementary Plants
- Purple leaf plum looks nice as a focal point in an otherwise green setting.
- Use in a landscape with other red- or purple-leaved plants, such as loropetalum and the purple-leaved forms of barberry.

## Recommended Selections
- 'Atropurpurea' is the most widely available, with ruby-red new leaves, turning wine-colored, then becoming dark reddish purple.
- 'Hollywood' has green leaves that turn deep-purple.
- 'Purpusii' has variegated leaves with white edges.

# Redbud

*Cercis canadensis*

## A Real Beauty We Often Take for Granted

The redbud with its heart-shaped leaves stands out as beautifully in a landscape as it does in the forest. The bright-pink-purple blooms that emerge on bare twigs before almost any other flowering tree are an early herald of spring. As summer progress, the tree develops interesting seedpods, which are eaten by birds and forest animals. Adventurous gardeners report the flowers are quite tasty when added to salads and that the seedpods can be made into fritters.

## Top Reasons to Plant

○ Beautiful, showy spring blooms
○ Graceful shape
○ Large, heart-shaped leaves in summer
○ Small size fits most yards
○ Tolerates variety of soil types
○ Grows well in partial sun

## Useful Hint

As with dogwoods, keep lawn mowers and string trimmers from damaging the trunk—such damage allows borers and diseases to enter.

## Bloom Color
Pink-purple or white

## Bloom Period
Spring

## Height/Width
20 to 35 feet x 25 to 35 feet

## Planting Location
- Prefers moist, well-drained soil with organic matter but adapts to most soil types, except those that stay wet
- Sun or light sun

## Planting
- Plant in midautumn or early spring.
- Dig the hole as deep as the rootball and three times as wide.
- Pulverize all clods and the bottom of the hole using a spade.
- Place the tree in the hole.
- Fill with dirt removed from the hole.
- Water thoroughly.
- Mulch with 2 inches of pine straw or wood chips.

## Watering
- Regular water is essential.
- Water when rainfall measures less than an inch in any week during the growing season.

## Fertilizing
- Fertilize in spring after the leaves have opened fully and again in late June using 2 tablespoons of 10-10-10 fertilizer for every foot of plant height.
- Once the tree reaches its desired height, fertilize only in the spring.

## Easy Tip

The redbud's pods provide food for wildlife, but they're messy when they fall—don't plant a redbud close to a driveway, sidewalk, or patio unless you enjoy slipping and sliding.

## Suggestions for Vigorous Growth
- Maintain a wide circle of mulch around the trunk to prevent mechanical injury from mowers or trimmers.
- If pruning is needed, do it in winter or after flowering.

## Pest Control
- Caterpillars may be a problem—control them with Bt (*Bacillus thuringiensis*).

## Complementary Plants
- Underplant with early-flowering spring bulbs in companionable colors.

## Recommended Selections
- 'Forest Pansy' has intensely purple leaves in spring that fade to dark-green in summer.
- 'Alba' has white flowers.
- 'Silver Cloud' has irregular variegation on its leaves and grows much better in shade than in full sun.

# Red Maple

*Acer rubrum*

## A Beautiful Shade Tree That's Red in Spring and Fall

Red maples mark the beginning of spring. Their red flowers emerge in clusters along the branches in mid-February before their leaves appear. Red maples also mark the end of the growing season with fiery-red leaves that stand out brilliantly against the yellow leaves of tulip poplars and the green needles of pine trees. A red maple is an excellent choice for a shade tree. It grows fast and doesn't have the weak limb structure of a silver maple.

## Top Reasons to Plant

- Red blooms in spring
- Red foliage in fall
- Graceful, spreading habit
- Pest and disease resistant
- Fast growing
- Attractive in three seasons
- Tolerates wet soil

## Useful Hint

The roots of the red maple will adapt to wet conditions by running along the surface of the ground, so avoid planting one near a sidewalk or drive.

## Bloom Color
Red

## Bloom Period
Spring

## Height/Width
40 to 60 feet x 30 to 50 feet

## Planting Location
- Prefers moist, well-drained, slightly acidic soil, but does well in average soil and wet areas
- Sun

## Planting
- Plant in fall or early spring.
- Dig the hole 6 feet wide and 1 foot deep, thoroughly breaking up the soil.
- Place the tree in the hole with the top of the rootball level with or a little higher than ground level.
- Fill with soil dug from the hole.
- If planting in spring, form a raised "doughnut" of soil around the outer edge of the rootball to concentrate water in the root area.
- Water thoroughly.
- Mulch with 2 inches of wood chips.

## Watering
- This tree needs water spring through fall—water deeply if rainfall doesn't total an inch per week.

## Fertilizing
- Do not fertilize until the tree has been in the ground for three months.
- While the tree is young, apply 2 tablespoons of 10-10-10 fertilizer in spring, summer, and fall.

# Easy Tip

Buy a named cultivar of red maple to ensure you have good fall color—the common red maple doesn't always have pretty fall color.

## Suggestions for Vigorous Growth
- Prune as needed to create three or four main limbs evenly spaced around the trunk, each 3 to 5 feet from the ground.
- Do not cut the growing tip of the main trunk—weak limbs may sprout and crash to the ground during a windstorm.

## Pest Control
- Purple eye leaf spot disease results in groups of purple "eyes" on leaves, and leaf galls may cause warty bumps on leaf surfaces—either can be prevented, but neither causes a decline in tree health.

## Complementary Plants
- Red maple makes an excellent specimen tree placed where it can be seen in spring and fall from indoors.

## Recommended Selections
- 'October Glory' and 'Red Sunset'® are easy to find and have fabulous fall foliage.
- 'Columnare' grows much narrower than other red maples, almost like a 'Bradford' pear.

# River Birch

*Betula nigra*

## A Versatile Tree with Fabulous Bark

A river birch is an excellent specimen tree when planted in the center of a landscape. Three single-trunked birches planted in a group make a better statement than one birch planted by itself, but on a small lot, a single-stemmed plant may be the best choice. The grayish white bark of river birch peels away from the trunk in paper-thin layers, revealing brown bark beneath—an attractive effect in winter.

## Top Reasons to Plant

○ Gorgeous peeling bark
○ Graceful shape
○ Grows well in wet clay soil
○ Tolerates variety of growing conditions
○ Disease and pest resistant
○ Good fall color on some cultivars

## Useful Hint

The river birch is the only type of birch that can stand the heat of Georgia's summers.

## Bloom Color
Grown for its foliage and bark

## Height/Width
20 to 50 feet x 20 to 30 feet

## Planting Location
- Prefers moist, acidic soil but adapts to any fertile soil other than alkaline, especially if watered
- Sun or mostly sun

## Planting
- Plant in fall after the weather has begun to cool.
- Dig the hole as deep as the rootball and three to five times as wide.
- Add 1 cup of lime and 1 tablespoon of 0-46-0 fertilizer per foot of hole diameter.
- Place the tree in the hole and fill with soil from the hole.
- Water thoroughly.
- Mulch with 2 inches of pine straw or wood chips.

## Watering
- Keep soil moist during the growing season.

## Fertilizing
- Feed in March and in midsummer with 2 tablespoons of 10-10-10 fertilizer for every foot of plant height.
- Once the tree reaches full height, no fertilizer is needed.

## Suggestions for Vigorous Growth
- In dry soils, maintain a 3-inch mulch.
- If you don't water in dry summer months, as many as half the leaves may fall—this usually isn't a major problem.

## Easy Tip
The river birch tolerates areas that don't drain well, but after a few years of growth, it can also stand considerable dryness.

- If necessary, prune in summer—river birch "bleeds" if a branch is cut in spring, which isn't harmful but is messy and discolors the bark.
- To expose the peeling white bark of river birch, remove the tree's lower limbs when it grows tall.
- If leaves are yellow rather than green during the summer, have the soil tested and add lime to bring the pH above 6.0 if indicated by the test.

## Pest Control
- Leaf spot may cause the leaves on common river birches to drop in hot, wet weather, but 'Heritage' river birch resists this problem.

## Complementary Plants
- River birch is the perfect choice for shading a gazebo that overlooks a backyard koi pond.

## Recommended Selections
- 'Heritage' is an excellent selection, with whiter bark than the common river birch and dark-green leaves.

# Sassafras
*Sassafras albidum*

## An Outstanding Native Tree for Fall Color

This native tree can't be beat for fall color—its lobed leaves turn to yellow, deep-orange, scarlet, and purple, putting on a stunning show. Its irregular shape gives the tree an interesting appearance in winter. In spring, fragrant yellow flowers outline the branches. And in September, female trees bear dark-blue fruits on scarlet stalks that are quite showy if you get to see them before the birds nab them.

## Top Reasons to Plant

○ Showy fall color
○ Fall fruit attracts birds
○ Adapts to variety of conditions
○ Pest and disease resistant
○ Pleasant scent
○ Handsome bark

## Useful Hint

Prune off sucker growth around the base in winter if you want to develop a single-trunked tree.

## Bloom Color
Yellow

## Bloom Period
Spring

## Height/Width
30 to 60 feet x 25 to 40 feet

## Planting Location
• Moist, acidic, well-drained soil
• Sun or partial shade

## Planting
• Plant balled-and-burlapped trees in early spring.
• Dig the hole three times as wide as and as deep as the rootball.
• Set the tree in the hole and remove any burlap, wire, or twine.
• Fill with soil taken from the hole.
• Water thoroughly.
• Mulch with 2 inches of pine straw or wood chips.

## Watering
• Water deeply each week when the tree is young if an inch of rainfall hasn't fallen.
• Once the tree is established, it tolerates drought.

## Fertilizing
• No fertilizer is needed.

## Easy Tip
Sassafras has a deep taproot, so it is best planted when the tree is young using container-grown or balled-and-burlapped trees, not dug from the wild.

## Suggestions for Vigorous Growth
• Prune as needed in winter.
• Sucker growth tends to form around a mature tree, especially if roots are damaged by cultivation.
• Keep mulched year-round.
• If leaves turn yellowish in summer, it likely means chlorosis from soil that is not acidic enough—feed with fertilizer made for acid-loving trees.

## Pest Control
• No serious pests or diseases trouble this tree.

## Complementary Plants
• Combine with other natives in naturalized plantings.

## Recommended Selections
• Plant the species.

# Saucer and Star Magnolias

*Magnolia × soulangiana* and *Magnolia stellata*

## Spring Knockouts with Big, Bold Blooms If Mother Nature Is Kind

Saucer and star magnolias are loved by Georgia garden gamblers. Their blooms appear very early in spring, and if we're unlucky, unexpected freezing temperatures turn the flowers to brown mush overnight. Saucer magnolia has large 3- to 4-inch flowers that are usually a light pinkish white inside and darker pink or purple outside. Star magnolia is a large shrub that can be pruned into a small tree with 3-inch, pure-white, fragrant blooms.

## Top Reasons to Plant

- Showy February blooms
- Graceful shape
- Attractive in winter
- Disease and pest resistant
- Can be trained as tree or multitrunked shrub
- Fragrant flowers

## *Useful Hint*

Mother Nature can be your enemy with these trees—causing unseasonably warm weather that encourages blooming followed by a hard frost that kills the flowers.

## Bloom Color
Pink, purplish, or white

## Bloom Period
Early spring

## Height/Width
Saucer magnolia: 20 to 30 feet x 15 to 25 feet
Star magnolia: 10 to 20 feet x 10 to 15 feet

## Planting Location
• Moist, well-drained, acidic soil containing organic matter
• Sun
• Sheltered from early spring winds

## Planting
• Plant in spring after last frost.
• Dig the hole as deep as the rootball and three to five times as wide.
• Add 1 cup of lime and 1 tablespoon of 0-46-0 fertilizer per foot of hole diameter.
• Place the tree in the hole and try to unwind the roots a little.
• Fill with soil from the hole.
• Water thoroughly.
• Mulch with 2 inches of pine straw or wood chips.

## Watering
• Water deeply whenever rainfall has been less than an inch in any week, especially in very hot weather.

## Fertilizing
• While the tree is young, feed it in March, May, and September with 1 cup of 10-10-10 fertilizer for each inch of trunk thickness measured 4 feet above the ground.

## Easy Tip
If you're impatient, these are the flowering trees for you—they typically have full-sized blossoms when only 3 feet tall.

## Suggestions for Vigorous Growth
• Maintain year-round mulch to keep the soil moist.
• Prune just after flowering, if needed, to develop a tree form—one trunk with four or five main branches
• In July, remove any small, spindly branches along the trunk.

## Pest Control
• Few insects and diseases trouble this tree.

## Complementary Plants
• Choose several of these trees with varying flower colors, and place them in different areas of the yard.

## Recommended Selections
• *Magnolia* x *soulangiana* 'Brozzonii' has huge (10-inch), mostly white flowers that appear later than the flowers of the species, avoiding frost damage.
• *Magnolia stellata* 'Royal Star' has pure-white flowers that emerge later than those of other star magnolias.

91

# Serviceberry

*Amelanchier* species and hybrids

## A Graceful Small Tree with Flowers and More

Like many native plants, serviceberry has collected a number of common names. Some people always call it sarvis tree. Others call it Juneberry for the dark little fruits in early summer (supposedly sweet and good for cooking, if you can get to them before the birds do). Serviceberry has clusters of white flowers in early spring. They're fleeting, but they're the sign that spring has truly sprung.

## Top Reasons to Plant

○ Beautiful flowers in spring
○ Fruit that attracts birds
○ Graceful, airy form
○ Grows moderately fast
○ Few insects or diseases
○ Excellent fall color
○ Turf grows underneath

## Useful Hint

*Amelanchier arborea* is the tree species most commonly available to gardeners, although Allegheny serviceberry (*Amelanchier laevis*) is often found in the wild.

## Bloom Color
White

## Bloom Period
Early spring

## Height/Width
15 to 30 feet x 20 to 30 feet

## Planting Location
- Prefers moist, acidic, well-drained soil, but tolerates many soil types
- Sun or partial shade

## Planting
- Plant container-grown or balled-and-burlapped trees in spring or fall.
- Dig the hole three times as wide as and as deep as the rootball.
- Place the tree at the same depth it grew before.
- Fill the hole with soil removed from it.
- Water well.
- Mulch with 2 inches of pine straw or wood chips.

## Watering
- In early years, water in those weeks when there isn't an inch of rainfall.
- Established trees should cope with mild dry spells.
- Water deeply in weeks with temperatures about 95 degrees Fahrenheit.

## Fertilizing
- Fertilizer is not usually needed.

## *Easy Tip*
Pay attention to serviceberry's eventual spread if you decide to grow it as a multistemmed shrub rather than a tree—it takes a lot of room.

## Suggestions for Vigorous Growth
- If pruning is needed, do it in spring after blooming has finished.
- Maintain mulch year-round, especially in dry weather.

## Pest Control
- Few insects or diseases trouble this tree.

## Complementary Plants
- Plant with spring wildflowers along the edge of woods.
- Pair with shadbush (*Amelanchier canadensis*), a shrub form with excellent fall color.

## Recommended Selections
- 'Autumn Brilliance' has very red fall foliage and grows fast.
- 'Princess Diana' displays spectacular red leaves in fall.

# Sourwood
*Oxydendrum arboreum*

## *An Easy-to-Grow Native That Looks Exotic and Unusual*

Sourwood is so exotic looking that it's easy to imagine it came from some inaccessible place on the other side of the world. Instead, it's an easy-to-grow American native most of us take for granted. At every season, sourwood calls attention to its unusual beauty with 10-inch clusters of creamy, bell-shaped flowers in summer, followed in autumn by ivory seed capsules hanging from the tips of the branches. Plus it has the most brilliant scarlet foliage in the fall forest.

## Top Reasons to Plant

- Long clusters of creamy flowers in summer
- Strands of ivory seed capsules in fall
- Brilliant scarlet leaves in fall
- Attractive pyramidal shape
- Few pests and diseases
- Needs little care

## *Useful Hint*

Although sourwood tolerates some shade, its blooms and fall color are much better in full sun.

## Bloom Color
Cream

## Bloom Period
Summer

## Height/Width
25 to 50 feet x 15 to 20 feet

## Planting Location
• Acidic, well-drained soil
• Sun

## Planting
• Plant in a prominent spot in early fall or spring.
• Dig the hole as deep as the rootball and three times as wide.
• Fill the hole with soil removed from it.
• Water with transplant solution.
• Mulch with 2 inches of pine straw or wood chips, but don't let the mulch touch the trunk.

## Watering
• When the tree is young, water well during dry spells.
• Once mature, sourwood can tolerate some dryness.
• Water small- and medium-sized trees during droughts or when temperatures are 95 degrees Fahrenheit or higher.

## Fertilizing
• Fertilizer is not needed unless the tree is not growing well.
• If necessary, apply high-nitrogen tree fertilizer in autumn after the leaves have fallen.

## *Easy Tip*
Sourwood blooms at a time when few other trees do.

## Suggestions for Vigorous Growth
• Little pruning is needed.
• Slow growth is normal.

## Pest Control
• Few serious insects or diseases bother this tree.

## Complementary Plants
• Plant sourwood in a place where it can show off its exotic looks and early autumn color.
• Use against an evergreen backdrop.

## Recommended Selections
• 'Chameleon' is a kaleidoscope of fall color with leaves turning from green to yellow, red, and purple, often with all colors at once.

# Southern Magnolia

*Magnolia grandiflora*

## The Quintessential Southern Belle of Trees

Only the flowering dogwood may be more strongly associated with the South than the magnolia. Its huge, fragrant white flowers appear in June, and from the 1930s to the 1960s, no high school prom in Georgia was complete without magnolia flower centerpieces on the tables. Children appreciate some of the less celebrated aspects of a magnolia. Its drooping branches make wonderful secret rooms, and the branches are spaced perfectly for climbing.

## Top Reasons to Plant

○ Huge creamy-white blossoms
○ Fragrant flowers
○ Shiny evergreen foliage
○ Attractive seedpods with red seeds
○ Few pests and diseases
○ Good cut flower
○ Good cut foliage for winter holiday decorations

## Bloom Color
White

## Bloom Period
Late spring and early summer

## Height/Width
40 to 70 feet x 20 to 40 feet

## Planting Location
• Rich, moist, acidic, well-drained soil
• Sun
• Protected from winter winds, if possible

## Planting
• Plant in midautumn or early spring.
• Dig the hole three to five times as wide as and as deep as the rootball.
• Add 1 cup of lime and 1 tablespoon of 0-46-0 fertilizer per foot of hole diameter.
• Set the tree in the hole and cut away all burlap, twine, or wire.
• Fill the hole with soil.
• Water well.
• Mulch with 2 inches of pine straw or wood chips.

## Watering
• Water deeply when rainfall is below normal.

## Fertilizing
• While the tree is young, feed it in March, May, and September with 1 cup

## Easy Tip

For a creative holiday decoration, wrap your magnolia with bright lights and work a bright star mounted on the appropriate length of metal conduit up the trunk to the top of the tree.

of 10-10-10 fertilizer for each inch of trunk thickness measured 4 feet above the ground.

## Suggestions for Vigorous Growth
• Prune in early spring if needed.
• Leave lower limbs to preserve the tree's graceful look and to hide its debris.

## Pest Control
• Few insect or disease problems bother this tree.

## Complementary Plants
• Southern magnolia makes a good backdrop for summer-flowering trees, such as chaste tree, and shrubs, such as smokebush.

## Recommended Selections
• 'Bracken's Brown Beauty' has rather small leaves that grow densely on the tree.
• 'Little Gem' is the best compact tree, with flowers in its first year and an eventual height of only 10 to 20 feet.

# Sweet Bay Magnolia
*Magnolia virginiana*

## A Smaller, Moisture-Loving Cousin of Southern Magnolia with Its Own Charms

Nothing beats the smell of magnolias blooming during late spring and summer. And unlike southern magnolia, which often dominates the landscape, sweet bay magnolia blends right in. It works well as a patio tree or in other limited spaces. Deciduous (losing its leaves in winter) in cold areas, sweet bay is mostly evergreen in the South. It does well in swampy, wet soils, and even allows turf to grow beneath its branches.

## Top Reasons to Plant

- Beautiful creamy-white flowers
- Fragrant blossoms
- Much smaller than southern magnolia
- Good for small yards and gardens
- Tolerates wet soil
- Attractive seedpods
- Good cut flower

## Bloom Color
Creamy-white

## Bloom Period
Spring to summer

## Height/Width
20 to 40 feet x 15 to 25 feet

## Planting Location
• Best in moist, fertile soil
• Sun, with some shade in the hottest part of the day

## Planting
• Plant in early fall or spring.
• Dig the hole three times as wide as and the same depth as the rootball.
• Add 1 cup of lime and 1 tablespoon of 0-46-0 fertilizer per foot of hole diameter.
• Place the tree in the hole and cut away any burlap, twine, or wire.
• Fill the hole and water well.
• Mulch with 2 inches of pine straw or wood chips.

## Watering
• Water regularly and do not let the soil dry out—sweet bay does not tolerate drought.

## *Easy Tip*

Consistently moist soil is the key to success with sweet bay magnolia—its other common name is swamp magnolia.

## Fertilizing
• Feed three times yearly with a slow-release, granular azalea fertilizer, making the first application as leaves emerge, the second application ten weeks later, and the third application in early fall.

## Suggestions for Vigorous Growth
• Prune only if necessary or to remove dead or damaged branches.

## Pest Control
• No significant pests or diseases bother this tree.

## Complementary Plants
• Plant among azaleas.
• Use in a ground-cover bed or with low-growing shrubs.

## Recommended Selections
• Plant the species.

## *Useful Hint*
Sweet bay is an excellent substitute for southern magnolia in smaller yards where soil is moist or watering easy.

# Sweet Gum

*Liquidambar styraciflua*

## *A Shade Tree with Leaves Beautiful in Summer and Fall*

Even children recognize the common sweet gum tree. They know from firsthand experience that prickly balls cover the ground beneath it. The five-pointed, star-shaped leaves are another way to quickly identify this fast-growing tree with beautiful fall color. The variety without gumballs makes an excellent shade tree for medium-sized to large landscapes.

## Top Reasons to Plant

- Beautiful red leaves in fall
- Attractive, unusual shape to leaves
- Excellent shade tree for large area
- Thrives in wet soil
- Few pests or diseases

## *Useful Hint*

If you want to plant a sweet gum but don't want the nuisance of the sticky balls, go for one of the "ball-less" cultivars—'Rotundiloba' is a good selection.

## Height/Width
50 to 80 feet x 30 to 50 feet

## Planting Location
- Best in moist or wet, acidic soils (leaves turn yellow in alkaline soils)
- Sun

## Planting
- Plant in midautumn or early spring.
- Dig the hole as deep as and three to five times as wide as the rootball.
- Add 1 cup of lime and 1 tablespoon of 0-46-0 fertilizer per foot of hole diameter.
- Place the tree in the hole and cut away any burlap, twine, or wire.
- Fill the hole with soil and water well.
- Mulch with 2 inches of pine straw or wood chips.

## Watering
- Keep the soil moist until the tree begins growing well—probably within a year or two.
- After the tree becomes established, water heavily in weeks when the temperature rises above 95 degrees Fahrenheit.

## Fertilizing
- While the tree is young, feed it in March, May, and September with 1 cup of 10-10-10 fertilizer for each inch of trunk thickness measured 4 feet above the ground.
- Once the tree matures, little fertilizer is needed.

## Suggestions for Vigorous Growth
- Do any required pruning at any time.
- If a young tree needs support, place a stake 18 inches away from both sides of the trunk, and stake the tree loosely enough that it can sway slightly.
- Young sweet gums occasionally send up sprouts from their base—remove these as they appear.

## Pest Control
- Caterpillars or scale may appear—use *Bacillus thuringiensis* (Bt) for caterpillars and a light horticultural oil (sometimes called "sun oil") to smother scale.

## Complementary Plants
- If one is a standout, two or three together in a small grove dazzle.

## Recommended Selections
- 'Rotundiloba' generally doesn't produce the balls for which sweet gum is famous.
- 'Gumball' is a bush form with a rounded top and straight sides, reaching only 8 feet high.

# Thornless Honey Locust

*Gleditsia triacanthos* f. *inermis*

## A Fine-Textured, Adaptable Tree with Light, Airy Foliage

Their drought resistance and adaptability to a range of suburban and city conditions account for the huge popularity of the honey locust as a yard specimen. Breeders have developed a thornless version with nice proportions and light, airy foliage. Featuring twenty to thirty small leaflets, the green leaves turn pale-yellow in autumn. In early summer, the scented flowers bloom an inconspicuous green, then give way to 8-inch-long pods later in the summer—unless you choose a type that has no pods.

## Top Reasons to Plant

○ Lovely, fine-textured foliage
○ Nice fall color
○ Drought tolerant when established
○ Turf grows beneath branches
○ Thrives in any well-drained soil

## Useful Hint

Be sure to choose a variety of honey locust with no thorns or pods.

## Bloom Color
Inconspicuous green flowers

## Bloom Period
Spring

## Height/Width
30 to 50 feet x 30 feet

## Planting Location
• Not fussy about soil type, as long as the soil is well drained
• Sun

## Planting
• Plant balled-and-burlapped trees in spring and container-grown ones anytime during the growing season.
• Dig the hole as deep as and three times as wide as the rootball.
• Add 1 cup of lime and 1 tablespoon of 0-46-0 fertilizer per foot of hole diameter.
• Place the tree in the hole so the top of the rootball is at soil level.
• Cut away any burlap, string, or wire and fill the hole with soil.
• Water well.
• Mulch with 2 inches of pine straw or wood chips.

## Watering
• Water regularly until established.

## Fertilizing
• No fertilizer is needed.

## Easy Tip
The airy, fine-textured foliage of honey locust permits grass to thrive beneath its branches.

## Suggestions for Vigorous Growth
• Maintain mulch year-round to keep soil moist and to reduce weeds.

## Pest Control
• Webworms (caterpillars) may appear— prune out their nests.

## Complementary Plants
• Thornless honey locust makes an excellent specimen tree in an open spot in the lawn.
• Plant along fence lines or property boundaries to be viewed from the house.

## Recommended Selections
• Cultivars with no seedpods or thorns include 'Halka'™, which is compact and rounded; 'Moraine', with deep-green foliage turning yellow in fall; 'Shademaster'®, which has a good form with ascending branches; and 'Sunburst', with golden spring foliage.

# Tulip Poplar

*Liriodendron tulipifera*

## A Native Beauty for a Large Setting

The beautiful tulip poplar is tall and majestic, the flowers are mildly fragrant, and the leaves turn yellow in autumn. But there's one problem—tiny tulip poplar tree seedlings are often given away to homeowners who have no clue how large they grow. This is one of our biggest native trees, suitable mostly for large properties. On one of those, it can be a magnificent sight.

## Top Reasons to Plant

- Tall, majestic tree for large areas
- Beautiful blooms
- Fragrant flowers
- Distinctive leaf shape
- Good fall color

## Useful Hint

If tulip poplar is a favorite of yours, but you have a small yard, look for some of the smaller cultivars now becoming available at nurseries.

## Bloom Color
Cream to yellow

## Bloom Period
Late spring to early summer

## Height/Width
70 to 100 feet x 35 to 55 feet

## Planting Location
• Moist, well-drained, slightly acidic soil
• Sun

## Planting
• Plant in spring.
• Dig the hole as deep as the rootball and three times as wide.
• Add 1 cup of lime and 1 tablespoon of 0-46-0 fertilizer per foot of hole diameter.
• Place the tree in the hole and cut away any burlap, string, or wire.
• Fill the hole with soil and water thoroughly.
• Mulch with 2 inches of pine straw or wood chips.

## Watering
• Moisture is essential—without it, leaves scorch and drop.
• Keep the soil moist at all times, especially when the tree is young and during dry weather or when temperatures rise above 95 degrees Fahrenheit.

## Fertilizing
• Do not fertilize unless the tree is not growing well.

*Easy Tip*

Place tulip poplar where it has plenty of room to grow—well away from power lines and buildings.

## Suggestions for Vigorous Growth
• Ensure that the soil receives adequate, regular moisture.

## Pest Control
• Numerous insect and disease problems plague this tree.
• Aphids are common, producing a sweet secretion often followed by black sooty mold—use a hose-end sprayer to wash off the mold, then spray the tree with insecticidal soap or light horticultural oil to get rid of the aphids.

## Complementary Plants
• Tulip poplar makes an excellent specimen tree; plant it where it can be admired and has room to grow.

## Recommended Selections
• Smaller cultivars include 'Ardis' and 'Compactum'.

# Winter King Hawthorn

*Crataegus viridis* 'Winter King'

## A Beautiful Small Tree with Spring Blooms, Fall Color, and Winter Fruit

'Winter King' overcomes the typical fungus diseases suffered by hawthorns. It has a broad vase shape and bears clusters of delicate white flowers in spring. After a show of bronze, red, and gold fall foliage, it reveals silvery bark patched with orange-brown and develops orange-red fruits that persist through winter. As you might expect, hawthorns are famous for their thorns, but 'Winter King' has sparse, small ones.

## Top Reasons to Plant

- Lovely branching structure
- Nice bark
- Beautiful white spring blooms
- Outstanding fall foliage
- Red fruits that last through winter
- Few pests and diseases
- Tolerates many soil types

## Useful Hint

Plant 'Winter King' where it can be viewed from inside during winter, when its bark and red fruits really show off.

106

## Bloom Color
White

## Bloom Period
Spring

## Height/Width
20 to 30 feet x 20 to 30 feet

## Planting Location
- Tolerates any soil but appreciates rich, deep soil
- Sun is best but tolerates some shade

## Planting
- Plant in spring.
- Dig the hole three times as wide as and as deep as the rootball.
- Add 1 cup of lime and 1 tablespoon of 0-46-0 fertilizer per foot of hole diameter.
- Set the tree in the hole so the rootball is level with the ground.
- Fill the hole with soil dug from it.
- Form a saucer with the soil to hold water and water well.
- Mulch with 2 inches of pine straw or wood chips.

## Watering
- Water new trees during the first year or two if rainfall is scarce.

## Fertilizing
- No fertilizer is needed if mulch is maintained year-round to decay and gently feed the tree.

## Suggestions for Vigorous Growth
- Keep mulched year-round to hold soil moisture.
- Young trees exposed to wind may need temporary staking.

*Easy Tip*

'Winter King' is well suited for only the northern half of the state—farther south, try the Washington hawthorn if you don't mind the thorns.

- Promptly prune off all suckers—'Winter King' is grafted onto the rootstock of the Washington hawthorn; suckers develop below the graft.
- Prune off any water sprouts (weak, suckering shoots) along branches.

## Pest Control
- Caterpillars, scale, or borers may attack stressed trees, so ensure 'Winter King' receives adequate water.

## Complementary Plants
- 'Winter King' is best used as a specimen tree—site it to be viewed from indoors and where it has plenty of room to spread and show its beautiful shape.

## Recommended Selections
- Washington hawthorn (*Crataegus phaenopyrum*), on whose roots 'Winter King' is grafted, is itself disease resistant and very attractive, but has thorns 1 to 3 inches long and is not suitable where there are children.

# Yellowwood

*Cladastris kentukea*

## A Gorgeous Spring Bloomer with Assets in Fall and Winter, Too

If you drive on highways in its native states of Tennessee, North Carolina, and Kentucky, you've probably admired this tree's long clusters of creamy flowers and wondered what it was. The flowers alone are reason enough to grow yellowwood, but it has many other fine qualities—bright-green leaves in summer that turn yellow in fall, smooth gray bark that adds winter interest to the yard, and an ability to grow in alkaline soil.

## Top Reasons to Plant

○ Pretty spring blooms
○ Good fall color
○ Nice winter bark
○ Tolerates wide variety of soils
○ Very winter hardy
○ No serious pests or diseases

## Useful Hint

Yellowwood is a nice patio or terrace tree due to its relatively small scale.

## Bloom Color
White or pink

## Bloom Period
Late spring

## Height/Width
30 to 60 feet x 40 to 50 feet

## Planting Location
- Well-drained acidic or alkaline soil
- Sun

## Planting
- Plant in spring.
- Dig the hole three times as wide as and as deep as the rootball.
- Add 1 cup of lime and 1 tablespoon of 0-46-0 fertilizer per foot of hole diameter.
- Place the tree in the hole and cut away any burlap, twine, or wire.
- Fill the hole with soil.
- Water thoroughly.
- Mulch with 2 inches of pine straw or wood chips.

## Watering
- Regular watering promotes faster growth.
- Keep the soil moist while the tree is young.
- As the tree ages, water when rainfall hasn't totaled an inch per week—though yellowwood tolerates some dryness.

## Fertilizing
- Fertilizing promotes faster growth.
- Feed with 1 pound of granular 19-0-0 fertilizer per inch of trunk diameter in late autumn.

## Easy Tip
Once established, yellowwood can tolerate some drought.

## Suggestions for Vigorous Growth
- When the tree is young, remove limbs with narrow crotches (limbs that join the trunk at a narrow angle rather than a wide one).
- Prune storm damage as soon as possible after it occurs.
- Do all other pruning in summer—in spring, this tree "bleeds" sap, which is messy and disturbing to watch, although not harmful.

## Pest Control
- No significant pests or diseases trouble this tree.

## Complementary Plants
- Grow as a shade tree or a lawn specimen.

## Recommended Selections
- 'Rosea' has fragrant, light-pink flowers.

# Yoshino Cherry
*Prunus × yedoensis*

## A Spectacular Flowering Cherry Like a Luminous White Cloud

Yoshino cherry is another of the spectacular flowering cherries brought over from Japan in the early 1900s. In spring, abundant white flowers cover the ends of the branches, appearing before the leaves do. Yoshino cherry flowers are fragrant, smelling slightly of almonds. This is the cherry that surrounds the Tidal Basin in Washington, D.C.—some years actually blooming during the Cherry Blossom Festival.

## Top Reasons to Plant

○ Gorgeous spring blooms
○ Fragrant flowers
○ Graceful branching habit
○ Relatively small size
○ Good cut flowers
○ Nice fall color on some cultivars

## Bloom Color
White or pale-pink

## Bloom Period
Spring

## Height/Width
20 to 30 feet x 25 to 40 feet

## Planting Location
- Fertile, well-drained soil with organic matter
- Sun

## Planting
- Plant in midautumn or early spring.
- Dig the hole as deep as the rootball and three to five times as wide.
- Add 1 cup of lime and 1 tablespoon of 0-46-0 fertilizer per foot of hole diameter.
- Place the tree in the hole and cut away any burlap, twine, or wire.
- Fill with soil dug from the hole.
- Water well.
- Mulch lightly.

## Watering
- Water when rainfall is less than an inch per week.
- To avoid root rot, be careful not to overwater in clay soil.

## *Easy Tip*

If you must plant Yoshino cherry in a low spot, first add 6 cubic feet of topsoil to the planting area to keep the roots out of wet soil.

## Fertilizing
- While the tree is young, feed it in March, May, and September with 1 cup of 10-10-10 fertilizer for each inch of trunk thickness measured 4 feet above the ground.

## Suggestions for Vigorous Growth
- Prune if needed as soon as flowers fade.
- Maintain a light mulch to protect the trunk from damage by lawn equipment.

## Pest Control
- Flowering cherries are subject to several pests and diseases—if any appear, consult the Extension Service.

## Complementary Plants
- Plant with azalea, rhododendron, and dogwood.
- Underplant with white or pale-pink spring bulbs.

## Recommended Selections
- 'Akebono' is smaller than Yoshino, and its flowers are soft-pink rather than white.
- 'Shidare Yoshino' has gracefully arching branches that "weep" to the ground.

## *Useful Hint*

If you find a Yoshino cherry with a swollen knot about 4 inches from ground level, it was grafted. Since the lower cherry rootstock can send up sprouts quite unlike the Yoshino, it is best to buy trees produced by rooted cuttings.

# Gardening Basics

We often tell beginning gardeners that if they haven't moved a plant three times, it's probably not yet in the right place. We take comfort in what our friend, nurseryman Bud Heist, says: "Don't say we can't grow it, just say we don't yet know what it needs."

Before you consider the light, drainage, and exposure in your favorite garden spot, spend a little time learning about the soil, nutrients, pests, and plant diseases common in your area.

## *Soil*

Some roots are reputed to be able to crack a house foundation or to break up a sidewalk, but roots are actually quite tender. When you put a plant in the soil, whether it is Bermuda grass or a baby oak, the roots will grow in the direction where resistance is least. Roots grow in the parts of the soil that offer moisture, oxygen, and nutrients.

Plants prefer to grow in soil that is a blend of clay, sand, and organic matter. The water and oxygen required by roots are plentiful in such an environment, and nutrients are available throughout. But few gardeners are blessed with perfect soil. The clay soil so abundant in north Georgia tends to have lots of moisture but little oxygen. The sandy soil prevalent along the coast has lots of oxygen but holds little water and few nutrients. The quickest way to make your soil better is to add more nutrients in the form of compost or other organic matter.

### Organic Matter

Organic matter is found in manure, compost, and other materials. Ground pine bark is a common soil amendment found throughout the state of Georgia. Gardeners in the southern part of the state use ground peanut hulls. Peat moss is readily available, but it doesn't seem to persist in our soil as long as the coarser materials do. You may purchase your organic soil amendments, but if you learn how to produce them from good compost or if you find a good source of manure, you can have an unlimited free supply of organic matter.

### Compost

Ever wonder why good gardeners wax eloquent about manure and compost? It's because either element, when added to a garden, can double the size and vigor of the plants. Some gardeners swear they achieve triple success when they add one of these materials to their ordinary soil. You might say that successful gardeners don't have green thumbs, they have black thumbs...from all of the manure and compost they've handled!

The reason compost is superior to any other source of organic matter is that it is *alive*. Compost is the decomposed remains of leaves, lawn clippings, pruned branches, and discarded stalks. The billions of fungi, bacteria, and other living creatures in compost are important parts of any healthy soil. Unfortunately, if you are gardening in a spot that is hard and bare, the soil has very little life in it. Plants growing in hard soil can be made beautiful, but they require more fertilizer and water to keep them looking their best.

Compost is the lazy gardener's friend. It contains billions of living creatures that help roots absorb water and nutrients. These tiny gardeners can take over some of the tasks of fertilizing and watering your plants.

Making compost never has to be complicated. Mother Nature has been composting for millions of years, and she never used a pitchfork or compost bin or expensive compost starter. Some gardeners choose to compost on a large scale, lugging bags of their neighbors' leaves up the street to dump on their compost piles. Others just throw their own leaves and clippings onto a pile and let nature take its course. Either method is fine. But the forming of compost does take time. It takes approximately six months and a thirty-gallon bag of yard trimmings to manufacture one cubic foot of compost. Mixing and turning a compost pile once a month can make the process go a bit faster.

While it's easy to make compost, it might be even easier to buy soil amendments at a garden center. But how much of this supplemental material does one need to make a difference in the soil? Dr. Tim Smalley, Professor of Horticulture at the University of Georgia, recommends spreading a layer of compost two inches thick over a garden flower bed and then mixing it with the soil underneath. In practical terms, that's two cubic feet of soil conditioner for every eight square feet of flower bed. You can see why composters are caught "borrowing" their neighbors' leaves at night!

The organic matter should be mixed to a depth of six to eight inches in the soil. With the addition of organic matter the soil will loosen, and it will stay loose for years. Oxygen will penetrate to where the roots are growing. The organic matter will absorb excess water and hold it in reserve for the plant to use when drier times come.

## Watering

It seems simple enough to water an outdoor plant, but most gardeners either overwater or underwater their plants. Proper watering is accomplished differently in different parts of the state. Sandy soil drains so well that water must be applied twice a week during a blistering summer. Clay soil holds too much water. Plants in clay soil must be watered less often, or they will succumb to root rot.

The amount of water to use also differs among plants. A shallow-rooted fern might need one-fourth gallon of water applied every other day. A densely rooted lawn requires six hundred gallons per thousand square feet every week. A new tree might require three gallons twice a week for one month and afterwards only need watering when a drought occurs.

Your own observations are best when you are determining when and how much to water. Here are some tips to get you started:

- Water container plants until the water runs out the bottom.
- Do not water again until the top inch of soil is dry.
- Put a hose at the base of a newly installed plant and thoroughly soak the root ball once a week. As the plant begins to grow larger, take into consideration that the size of the root zone will also increase.
- Use shallow cans to measure the amount of water applied by your lawn sprinkler. Put six cans in the area being sprinkled and run the system for an hour. Then measure the depth of water in all of the cans. If the average depth of water is one-half inch, you will know the grass root zone has been irrigated. This may take one to two hours.
- If summer restrictions limit your watering, determine which plants would cost the most to replace, and water them first. It makes more sense to save a specimen maple tree than to keep ten dollars worth of petunias alive.
- An inexpensive water timer and a few soaker hoses can be a gardener's best friends.

### Mulch

If a plant's roots are subjected to a long Georgia drought, even the toughest plant in the finest soil will suffer. Mulching will help you avoid this problem. Georgia's millions of pine trees give us two of the best mulches in the world, pine straw and pine bark chips. Mulch acts like a blanket. It keeps moisture in the soil, and it prevents plant roots from becoming too hot or too cold. Other good mulches include shredded fall leaves, wood chips, and shredded cypress bark. Few gardeners succeed without placing a one- to two-inch layer of mulch on top of the soil around all of their plants.

## *Nutrients*

Plants need nitrogen, phosphorus, and potassium in order to grow well. When you buy a bag of fertilizer, you will see three numbers on the label. These numbers indicate the amounts of nitrogen, phosphorus, and potassium in the fertilizer. The numbers represent the percentage of each nutrient in the mixture. For example, a bag of 10-10-10 fertilizer contains 10% nitrogen (N), 10% phosphorus (P), and 10% potassium (K). The other 70% is just clay.

Each nutrient serves a function in the overall good health of a plant. So how do you know which fertilizer to buy when your garden center offers dozens of combinations of the three nutrient numbers? Just look at the numbers on the bag and remember: Up, Down, and All Around.

Up: Nitrogen promotes leaf growth. That's why lawn fertilizer has a high nitrogen percentage. A common turf fertilizer is a 16-4-8, but some brands have even more nitrogen than this. Grass leaves are mowed off constantly, so nitrogen is needed to help grow more of them.

**Down**: Phosphorus is important in the formation of roots and is very important for flower, seed, and fruit growth. That's why so-called "starter fertilizers" and "bloom fertilizers" have high percentages of phosphorus.

**All Around**: Potassium increases overall cell health. When your plant is under stress from drought or from cold, adequate potassium helps the plant withstand the crisis. "Winterizer" fertilizer for lawns is a good choice for grass that must endure such conditions. Its potassium percentage is high to help the grass fight winter cold damage.

It is not necessary to buy a different fertilizer for each of the plant types you have in your landscape. You really can't hurt a plant by applying the wrong fertilizer. Your perennials won't be damaged by the application of "azalea fertilizer." The lawn won't be hurt if you fertilize it with 10-10-10. There may be some situations in which one type of fertilizer is marginally better; for example, a "slow-release turf fertilizer" might be especially desirable for some types of grass. But you can do quite well with the purchase of just three main types of fertilizer: 16-4-8 for your lawn, 6-12-12 for new plants, and 10-10-10 for everything else.

How do you know what amount of fertilizer to apply? How much nutrition does your soil already hold? Do you need any lime? To find out, you need to perform a soil test.

## Soil Test

There are two ways to test your soil. You can purchase an inexpensive gardener's test kit with simple chemicals and test tubes and do it yourself, or you can take some of your soil to your local county Extension Service office for a low-cost analysis.

Test kits are economical and simple to use. To use one, you'll mix your soil with water, then add a few drops of indicator chemical that will cause the water to change color. If you feel confident that you can match the color of the water with the colors on the small color wheel that is provided, you can determine which nutrients you need to add to your soil. If you don't trust your powers of analysis, you might want to compare your conclusions with those of the University of Georgia Soil Testing Laboratory through your local county Extension Service office.

Having soil tested by the Extension Service is a simple process as well. Collect several scoops of dirt from different areas of your yard and mix them together. The Extension Service needs just one cup of this soil mixture for the test. Put the soil in a bag, take it to your local Extension office, and tell the Extension agent what you intend to grow in it. The soil will be shipped to a laboratory in Athens. Within ten days you will receive a mailed report describing the nutrients present in your soil, the amounts in which they are present, and specific recommendations for correct fertilizer use.

## Lime

Though lime does not offer plant nutrients (aside from calcium, which plants need in small amounts), it helps plants absorb nutrients more efficiently. Georgia soils, particularly in the northern half of the state, tend to be acidic. In an acidic soil, plant roots can't collect the nitrogen, phosphorus, and potassium they need to function. Lime makes soil less acidic. Soil acidity is measured in numbers from 1 to 14 on what is called the pH scale. Most plants prefer soil that has a pH of 6.0 to 6.5. A hard clay subsoil may have a pH of 4.5. It takes a lot of lime to move the pH up to 6.5. Your soil test will determine the pH of your soil and the amount of lime it needs.

# *Pests and Diseases*

The same conditions that make our gardens so beautiful make Georgia a happy homeland for insect and disease pests. A long growing season means that insect populations have time to explode each year. Our high humidity and warm temperatures are perfect for the growth of fungi and bacteria.

It cannot be said often enough that a healthy plant is the best defense against pests. A plant that grows vigorously can quickly overcome insect damage. A plant that is not stressed by its environment can resist disease spores. Many of the plants included in this book were chosen because of their strong resistance to insects and diseases. If you follow our recommendations about the proper placement of your plants and how to care for them, your garden will rarely need pesticides. If you choose the plant varieties we recommend, you will have genetic allies in your fight against pests.

### Organic vs. Inorganic Gardening

If you find pests attacking your plants, what should you do? Is the problem bad enough to use a pesticide? Which pesticide should you use? Should you rely on synthetic chemicals or should you choose pesticides made from organic sources? These questions trouble all of us. Some gardeners prefer to use only organic pesticides. Others are more pragmatic, sometimes using synthetic pesticides, occasionally preferring organic ones, but always striving to use the smallest amounts possible in every case.

There is no single correct answer to the question: Which is best— organic or inorganic gardening? Synthetic pesticides for home gardeners have been repeatedly tested for safety by their manufacturers and by the federal government. Scientists and bureaucrats who advise us on environmental matters have declared that prudent use of approved pesticides offers fewer health risks than we would encounter if we avoided pesticides completely and endangered our food supply. Organic gardening does not always completely eliminate pesticide use, as it sometimes calls for the use of pesticides that come from organic sources. These organic pesticides may have risks higher or lower than synthetic ones. Fortunately, new gardening products with fewer risks appear on the market every year.

The choice between an "organic" or an "inorganic" garden is yours alone to make. You must decide whether the convenience of using synthetic pesticides offsets the hard work and constant vigilance required to completely eliminate their use.

### Information on Pesticide Use

If you need advice on which pesticides to use, the best resource for assistance is the local office of the University of Georgia Cooperative Extension Service. The agents there maintain the latest research data on the most effective and least potentially harmful pesticides to use. Ask them to tell you about all of the alternatives for solving your pest problem. Then you can use your experience and wisdom to make the choices that are best for your situation.

## The Name Game

Gardeners may wonder why they need to know the scientific names of plants. The answer is simple: you want to make sure the rose you purchase for your own garden is the same sweet-smelling rose you admired (and coveted) in your neighbor's garden. It's true that scientific names, which are derived from Latin or Greek, can be long and hard to pronounce. But unlike a common plant name, which often is applied to two very different plants, a scientific designation is specific and unique.

Throughout this book we identify plants by both their scientific and common names. A plant's scientific name consists of the genus (the first word) and an epithet. For example, all maples belong to the genus Acer. The epithet (in our example, rubrum) identifies a specific kind of maple. *Acer rubrum* is a red maple. The genus and epithet are always italicized and the genus name begins with a capital letter, while the entire epithet is always written in lower case.

A third word in the name may refer to a special variety of the plant, called a cultivar. The cultivar name is important because it designates a superior selection known for bigger blooms, better foliage, or some other noteworthy characteristic. A cultivar name is distinguished by the use of single quotation marks, as in the name Acer rubrum 'October Glory', a red maple with excellent fall leaf color. Most cultivars must be propagated by division or cuttings because they may not come true from seed.

A scientific name can change, but this happens only rarely, and there are certain rigid rules that apply to the practice of plant nomenclature. It is much easier to track down a wonderful plant if you know the full scientific name. Armed with a knowledge of both scientific and common names, you should be able to acquire the best plants for your Georgia garden.

## Propagation

Once you become excited about gardening, you may develop "plant lust." You'll start to think that you must buy every new and exciting plant you discover. A much less expensive way to acquire your plants is to propagate them using seeds, cuttings, or divisions.

Growing annuals from seed works well, but it is usually the slowest method for propagating perennials and is not always successful. The good news is that once they are well established in your garden, many perennial plants can be easily divided and transplanted, providing a constant supply of new plants.

When dividing a perennial, dig up the entire plant and separate it into pieces. You may dig up a mature clump and use a digging fork and your fingers to tease apart the roots, or you can make a clean cut with a straight-edged shovel to divide the large clump into smaller pieces. Make sure each piece has roots and buds. Remember, always have the new garden area prepared ahead of time for the new divisions, and don't let the roots dry out. Once all the divisions are planted, water them well. They'll grow large in no time!

Rooting stem cuttings is another option for propagating both perennials and annuals, as well as many shrubs. The important point to remember about cuttings is to take cuttings during the correct season. Timing is more important with shrubs than with perennials and annuals. Rooting stem cuttings provides a simple means to overwinter a piece of an annual that has grown too big to save in its present size; thus, it can be preserved and propagated again.

Another easy method for propagating plants, including most azaleas and hydrangeas, is layering. Penny McHenry, president of the American Hydrangea Society and a keen Atlanta gardener, propagates some of her favorite hydrangeas by bending young branches so they touch the ground. Making sure to loosen the dirt at the point of contact, she places soil and organic matter on top of the stem and uses a brick to weigh it down. Within two months, Penny has a newly rooted plant that can be cut off from the main plant and transplanted to a new location.

These are just a few suggestions for ways to get more out of your garden or to share your bounty with friends. Some of the most wonderful gardens started with "a piece of this and a division of that." Who knows, you may develop your own favorite technique for propagating a special rose or that mildew-resistant phlox you discover in your garden!

With these few tips you now have an overview of the basic information needed to become a gardener. To obtain the truly valuable skills of gardening, you will have to practice the 4-H Club motto: Learn by Doing. You will have to don your old jeans, take up your shovel, and dig!

If you keep your heart and mind open to the nuances of nature, you will cultivate more than just pretty flowers and strong trees. Both your plants and you yourself will grow in your beautiful garden. Fayetteville nurseryman Steven Stinchcomb may have said it best: "Some people are just gardeners in their heads and some people become gardeners in their hearts."

Good Gardening!

# Glossary

Alkaline soil: soil with a pH greater than 7.0. It lacks acidity, often because it has limestone in it.

All-purpose fertilizer: powdered, liquid, or granular fertilizer with a balanced proportion of the three key nutrients—nitrogen (N), phosphorus (P), and potassium (K). It is suitable for maintenance nutrition for most plants.

Annual: a plant that lives its entire life in one season. It is genetically determined to germinate, grow, flower, set seed, and die the same year.

Balled and burlapped: describes a tree or shrub grown in the field whose soilball was wrapped with protective burlap and twine when the plant was dug up to be sold or transplanted.

Bare root: describes plants that have been packaged without any soil around their roots. (Often young shrubs and trees purchased through the mail arrive with their exposed roots covered with moist peat or sphagnum moss, sawdust, or similar material, and wrapped in plastic.)

Barrier plant: a plant that has intimidating thorns or spines and is sited purposely to block foot traffic or other access to the home or yard.

Beneficial insects: insects or their larvae that prey on pest organisms and their eggs. They may be flying insects, such as ladybugs, parasitic wasps, praying mantids, and soldier bugs, or soil dwellers such as predatory nematodes, spiders, and ants.

Berm: a narrow, raised ring of soil around a tree, used to hold water so it will be directed to the root zone.

Bract: a modified leaf structure on a plant stem near its flower, resembling a petal. Often it is more colorful and visible than the actual flower, as in dogwood.

Bud union: the place where the top of a plant was grafted to the rootstock; usually refers to roses.

Canopy: the overhead branching area of a tree, usually referring to its extent including foliage.

Cold hardiness: the ability of a perennial plant to survive the winter cold in a particular area.

Composite: a flower that is actually composed of many tiny flowers. Typically, they are flat clusters of tiny, tight florets, sometimes surrounded by wider-petaled florets. Composite flowers are highly attractive to bees and beneficial insects.

Compost: organic matter that has undergone progressive decomposition by microbial and macrobial activity until it is reduced to a spongy, fluffy texture. Added to soil of any type, it improves the soil's ability to hold air and water and to drain well.

Corm: the swollen energy-storing structure, analogous to a bulb, under the soil at the base of the stem of plants such as crocus and gladiolus.

**Crown:** the base of a plant at, or just beneath, the surface of the soil where the roots meet the stems.

**Cultivar:** a CULTIvated VARiety. It is a naturally occurring form of a plant that has been identified as special or superior and is purposely selected for propagation and production.

**Deadhead:** a pruning technique that removes faded flower heads from plants to improve their appearances, abort seed production, and stimulate further flowering.

**Deciduous plants:** unlike evergreens, these trees and shrubs lose their leaves in the fall.

**Desiccation:** drying out of foliage tissues, usually due to drought or wind.

**Division:** the practice of splitting apart perennial plants to create several smaller-rooted segments. The practice is useful for controlling the plant's size and for acquiring more plants; it is also essential to the health and continued flowering of certain ones.

**Dormancy:** the period, usually the winter, when perennial plants temporarily cease active growth and rest. Dormant is the verb form, as used in this sentence: *Some plants, like spring-blooming bulbs, go dormant in the summer.*

**Established:** the point at which a newly planted tree, shrub, or flower begins to produce new growth, either foliage or stems. This is an indication that the roots have recovered from transplant shock and have begun to grow and spread.

**Evergreen:** perennial plants that do not lose their foliage annually with the onset of winter. Needled or broadleaf foliage will persist and continues to function on a plant through one or more winters, aging and dropping unobtrusively in cycles of three or four years or more.

**Floret:** a tiny flower, usually one of many forming a cluster, that comprises a single blossom.

**Foliar:** of or about foliage—usually refers to the practice of spraying foliage, as in fertilizing or treating with insecticide; leaf tissues absorb liquid directly for fast results, and the soil is not affected.

**Germinate:** to sprout. Germination is a fertile seed's first stage of development.

**Graft (union):** the point on the stem of a woody plant with sturdier roots where a stem from a highly ornamental plant is inserted so that it will join with it. Roses are commonly grafted.

**Hardscape:** the permanent, structural, nonplant part of a landscape, such as walls, sheds, pools, patios, arbors, and walkways.

**Herbaceous:** plants having fleshy or soft stems that die back with frost; the opposite of woody.

**Hybrid:** a plant that is the result of intentional or natural cross-pollination between two or more plants of the same species or genus.

**Low water demand:** describes plants that tolerate dry soil for varying periods of time. Typically, they have succulent, hairy, or silvery-gray foliage and tuberous roots or taproots.

**Mulch:** a layer of material over bare soil to protect it from erosion and compaction by rain, and to discourage weeds. It may be inorganic (gravel, fabric) or organic (wood chips, bark, pine needles, chopped leaves).

**Naturalize:** (*a*) to plant seeds, bulbs, or plants in a random, informal pattern as they would appear in their natural habitats; (*b*) to adapt to and spread throughout adopted habitats (a tendency of some nonnative plants).

**Nectar:** the sweet fluid produced by glands on flowers that attract pollinators such as hummingbirds and honeybees, for whom it is a source of energy.

**Organic material, organic matter:** any material or debris that is derived from plants. It is carbon-based material capable of undergoing decomposition and decay.

**Peat moss:** organic matter from peat sedges (United States) or sphagnum mosses (Canada), often used to improve soil texture. The acidity of sphagnum peat moss makes it ideal for boosting or maintaining soil acidity while also improving its drainage.

**Perennial:** a flowering plant that lives over two or more seasons. Many die back with frost, but their roots survive the winter and generate new shoots in the spring.

**pH:** a measurement of the relative acidity (low pH) or alkalinity (high pH) of soil or water based on a scale of 1 to 14, 7 being neutral. Individual plants require soil to be within a certain range so that nutrients can dissolve in moisture and be available to them.

**Pinch:** to remove tender stems and/or leaves by pressing them between thumb and forefinger. This pruning technique encourages branching, compactness, and flowering in plants, or it removes aphids clustered at growing tips.

**Pollen:** the yellow, powdery grains in the center of a flower. A plant's male sex cells, they are transferred to the female plant parts by means of wind or animal pollinators to fertilize them and create seeds.

**Raceme:** an arrangement of single-stalked flowers along an elongated, unbranched axis.

**Rhizome:** a swollen energy-storing stem structure, similar to a bulb, that lies horizontally in the soil, with roots emerging from its lower surface and growth shoots from a growing point at or near its tip, as in bearded iris.

**Rootbound (or potbound):** the condition of a plant that has been confined in a container too long, its roots having been forced to wrap around themselves and even swell out of the container. Successful transplanting or repotting requires untangling and trimming away of some of the matted roots.

**Root flare:** the transition at the base of a tree trunk where the bark tissue begins to differentiate and roots begin to form just before entering the soil. This area should not be covered with soil when planting a tree.

**Self-seeding:** the tendency of some plants to sow their seeds freely around the yard. It creates many seedlings the following season that may or may not be welcome.

**Semievergreen:** tending to be evergreen in a mild climate but deciduous in a rigorous one.

**Shearing:** the pruning technique whereby plant stems and branches are cut uniformly with long-bladed pruning shears (hedge shears) or powered hedge trimmers. It is used when creating and maintaining hedges and topiary.

**Slow-acting fertilizer:** fertilizer that is water insoluble and therefore releases its nutrients gradually as a function of soil temperature, moisture, and related microbial activity. Typically granular, it may be organic or synthetic.

**Succulent growth:** the sometimes undesirable production of fleshy, water-storing leaves or stems that results from overfertilization.

**Sucker:** a new-growing shoot. Underground plant roots produce suckers to form new stems and spread by means of these suckering roots to form large plantings, or colonies. Some plants produce root suckers or branch suckers as a result of pruning or wounding.

**Tuber:** a type of underground storage structure in a plant stem, analogous to a bulb. It generates roots below and stems above ground (example: dahlia).

**Variegated:** having various colors or color patterns. The term usually refers to plant foliage that is streaked, edged, blotched, or mottled with a contrasting color—often green with yellow, cream, or white.

**White grubs:** fat, off-white, wormlike larvae of Japanese beetles. They reside in the soil and feed on plant (especially grass) roots until summer when they emerge as beetles to feed on plant foliage.

**Wings:** (a) the corky tissue that forms edges along the twigs of some woody plants such as winged euonymus; (b) the flat, dried extension of tissue on some seeds, such as maple, that catch the wind and help them disseminate.

# Bibliography

Armitage, Allan. 1989. *Herbaceous Perennial Plants: A Treatise on Their Culture and Garden Attributes*. Varsity Press, Inc. Athens, GA.

Bender, Steven and Felder Rushing. 1993. *Passalong Plants*. The University of North Carolina Press. Chapel Hill, NC.

Brooklyn Botanic Garden. *Plants and Gardens Handbooks*, many different subjects. List available from Brooklyn Botanic Garden, 1000 Washington Ave., Brooklyn, NY.

Burke, Ken (ed.). 1980. *Shrubs and Hedges*. The American Horticultural Society. Franklin Center, PA.

Burke, Ken (ed.). 1982. *Gardening in the Shade*. The American Horticultural Society, Franklin Center, PA.

Dirr, Michael. 1990. *Manual of Woody Landscape Plants*. Stipes Publishing. Champaign, IL.

Gardiner, J.M. 1989. *Magnolias*. Globe Pequot Press, Chester, PA.

Gates, Galen et al. 1994. *Shrubs and Vines*. Pantheon Books. New York, NY.

Greenlee, John. 1992. *The Encyclopedia of Ornamental Grasses*. Rodale Press. Emmaus, PA.

Halfacre, R. Gordon and Anne R. Shawcroft. 1979. *Landscape Plants of the Southeast*. Sparks Press. Raleigh, NC.

Harper, Pamela and Frederick McGourty. 1985. *Perennials: How to Select, Grow and Enjoy*. HP Books. Tucson, AZ.

Heath, Brent and Becky. 1995. *Daffodils for American Gardens*. Elliott & Clark Publishing. Washington, DC.

Hipps, Carol Bishop. 1994. *In a Southern Garden*. Macmillan Publishing. New York, NY.

Lawrence, Elizabeth. 1991. *A Southern Garden*. The University of North Carolina Press. Chapel Hill, NC.

Lawson-Hall, Toni and Brian Rothera. 1996. *Hydrangeas*. Timber Press. Portland, OR.

Loewer, Peter. 1992. *Tough Plants for Tough Places*. Rodale Press. Emmaus, PA.

Mikel, John. 1994. *Ferns for American Gardens*. Macmillan Publishing. New York, NY.

Ogden, Scott. 1994. *Garden Bulbs for the South*. Taylor Publishing. Dallas, TX.

Still, Steven. 1994. *Manual of Herbaceous Ornamental Plants*. 4th edition. Stipes Publishing. Champaign, IL.

Vengris, Jonas and William A. Torello. 1982. *Lawns*. Thomson Publications. Fresno, CA.

Winterrowd, Wayne. 1992. *Annuals for Connoisseurs*. Prentice Hall. New York, NY.

# Photography Credits

Liz Ball and Rick Ray: pages 9, 11, 12, 14, 16, 18, 36, 42, 48, 56, 58, 60, 72, 76, 84, 90, 92, 106

Thomas Eltzroth: pages 8, 10, 20, 26, 28, 30, 32, 34, 40, 50, 62, 68, 70, 78, 80, 100, 102, 104

Jerry Pavia: pages 44, 54, 64, 66, 74, 82, 86, 88, 94

Pam Harper: pages 22, 24, 38, 52, 98, 110

Dr. Mike Dirr: page 108

Lorenzo Gunn: page 96

Andre Viette: page 46

# Plant Index

126

# Want to know more about Georgia gardening?

*Interested in fantastic flowers for Georgia? Do you want healthful and tasty herbs, fruits, and vegetables from your Georgia garden? How about stunning Georgia shrubs?*

If you enjoy *50 Great Trees for Georgia*, you will appreciate similar books featuring Georgia flowers, vegetables (including fruits and herbs), and shrubs. These valuable books also deserve a place in your gardening library.

### 50 Great Flowers for Georgia

Erica Glasener and Walter Reeves share their personal recommendations on fifty delightful flowering plants for Georgia. From colorful annuals that give you spring-to-fall color, to hard-working perennials that return year after year, you will find much to choose from in this book.

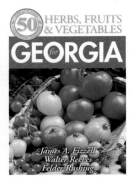

### 50 Great Herbs, Fruits and Vegetables for Georgia

If you are inclined to "edibles" in your Georgia garden, this is the book for you. It provides valuable advice on how to select, plant and grow tasty herbs, luscious fruits, and flavorful vegetables. Written by James A. Fizzell, Walter Reeves, and Felder Rushing, this book offers more than seventy-five years of gardening wisdom all in an easy to-use-format.

### 50 Great Shrubs for Georgia

If you want guidance on great shrubs for Georgia, this is the book for you. From the boxwood to the flowering azalea, Erica Glasener and Walter Reeves share their gardening insight on fifty wonderful shrubs for Georgia.

## Look for each of these books today.